Last Things

Banner Mini-Guides introduce the reader to some of the major themes and issues related to the Christian faith. They lay a solid foundation of Bible teaching while encouraging more thorough exploration of the theme with suggestions for further reading. The mini-guides will seamlessly fit into the teaching quarters of the church year with their thirteen-chapter format, making them useful for group as well as for individual study.

Last Things

Preparing for the Future in the Present

Banner Mini-Guides

Key Truths

David McKay

THE BANNER OF TRUTH TRUST

THE BANNER OF TRUTH TRUST

Head Office
3 Murrayfield Road
Edinburgh, EH12 6EL
UK

North America Office
610 Alexander Spring Road
Carlisle, PA 17015
USA

banneroftruth.org

ISBN
Print: 978 1 80040 353 6
Epub: 978 1 80040 354 3
Kindle: 978 1 80040 355 0

*

Typeset in 10/14 pt Minion Pro
at the Banner of Truth Trust, Edinburgh

Printed in the USA by
Versa Press, Inc.,
East Peoria, IL

Contents

Introduction: God Holds the Future   1

1. Facing Death   9
2. Beyond the Grave   17
3. The Coming of the Kingdom   25
4. The Signs of the Times   33
5. The Future of the Jewish People   49
6. The Promised Return of Christ   57
7. Our Resurrection Hope   65
8. Raised in Glory   73
9. Making Sense of 'the Rapture'   81
10. The Final Judgment   89
11. The Solemn Truth about Hell   97
12. Christians in the Final Judgment   105
13. The New Creation   113

Further Reading   127

Introduction:
God Holds the Future

Trying to know the future fascinates many people. They would love to know what lies ahead of them—or, at least, parts of it. Much of that interest is bound up with fear. Among the many fears that trouble the hearts and minds of men and women one of the most burdensome and most common is fear of the unknown. Most of us at some point in our lives fear that some sudden crisis or trial will come upon us unexpectedly and that we will be overwhelmed by it. The crisis that is feared could be the death of a loved one, a serious or even terminal illness, the loss of employment, a major financial loss, or any one of a long list of other potential disasters. Many think that if only they knew what was coming, they would be better able to cope.

From earliest times there have been those who claimed to be able to look into the future and probe its secrets. Astrologers, clairvoyants, mediums, shamans, and others have claimed to know what the future holds and have persuaded many to believe them. Far from being a relic of a superstitious past now discredited by 'science', this outlook is still with us. The New Age Movement in some of its multitude of forms has taken up ancient practices and dressed them in contemporary clothes—mediums have become 'channellers'—but the goal is the same. Even the newspaper horoscope has its devotees, though they might be reluctant to admit it.

Of course, not everyone wants to know the future, and probably nobody wants to know it fully. What if you discover that a coming crisis is something you can do nothing to avoid? Surely it would be better not to know? The recent growth in the science of genetics has made possible testing for various conditions which a person's genes may predispose him to develop. The question is now being asked, 'If there is no treatment for a particular condition, do I have a right not to know I am susceptible?'

Christians are not immune from curiosity about the future. Indeed, the Bible has a lot to say about it, both as far as individuals are concerned and also the universe as a whole. God's word does not provide individually tailored predictions about the future, nor does it answer all our questions, but it does provide answers—God's answers—to the really important questions. We will be looking at what the Bible says about 'eschatology'—the 'last things'—things that still lie in the future, including death, resurrection, the return of Christ, and the final judgment. Christians often hold different views about some of these issues but our aim will be to stick as closely as we can to what the Bible says and try to avoid speculation and guesswork.

To introduce our study of the last things we begin with the crucial truth: *God holds the future*. Three aspects of this truth should occupy our attention:

1. God is sovereign

It is sad that for some Christians the doctrine of the sovereignty of God is a baffling puzzle, whilst for others it is frightening and off-putting. There is something in the heart of every sinner that stirs a desire to control our lives, to be our own sovereign. Even when we are saved we tend to resist acknowledging God's sovereignty and to see it as a threat to our freedom.

In fact, the truth that God is sovereign over his whole creation is full of comfort and reassurance for his people. When a Christian looks at a world of suffering and chaos, where most of the major problems humanity faces are beyond the capacity even of world leaders to solve and where most aspects of our own lives are really beyond our control, he knows that someone is in control, and that someone is the God who reveals himself in the Bible.

We should take note of Paul's reference to 'the purpose of him who works all things according to the counsel of his will' (Eph. 1:11). The same wonderful truth is expressed by the humbled Babylonian king, Nebuchadnezzar: 'His dominion is an everlasting dominion, and his kingdom endures from generation to generation; all the inhabitants of the earth are accounted as nothing, and he does according to his will among the host of heaven and among the inhabitants of the earth; and none can stay his hand or say to him

3

"What have you done?"' (Dan. 4:34, 35). God's sovereignty is comprehensive, leaving nothing outside its scope. There is nowhere in the entire creation where 'chance' is lord or where 'luck' rules. In every place the Lord is sovereign.

The Bible describes the outworking of God's sovereignty in the 'big picture'—in the rise and fall of nations, not only in relation to Israel. Thus we are told in Amos 9:7 that the Lord brought Israel from Egypt, the Philistines from Caphtor, and the Syrians from Kir. Much of the material in the Old Testament prophetic books such as Isaiah and Jeremiah relates to the dealings of a sovereign God with the nations of the world he has made.

God's sovereignty also includes the 'small picture' of the details of life in his creation. A striking example is provided by Jesus in Matthew 10:29, 'Are not two sparrows sold for a penny? And not one of them will fall to the ground apart from your Father.' Even the most apparently insignificant aspects of the created world come under the direction of God's sovereign providence.

Notice also the Lord's statement that 'you are of more value than many sparrows' (Matt. 10:31). God's sovereignty extends to individual people. The Bible provides a multitude of examples, from Nebuchadnezzar on his throne (Dan. 4) to Joseph in prison (Gen. 41). The life of the Lord Jesus was directed at every point by God's sovereign will, not excluding the crucifixion 'according to the definite plan and foreknowledge of God' (Acts 2:23). Thus with regard to his own future the believer can say, 'My times are in your hand' (Psa. 31:15).

2. *God's plan is perfect*

The thought of someone exercising absolute sovereignty would be terrifying if it were in the hands of a mere human, ourselves included. We can recall the evil perpetrated by despots down through history, such as Hitler and Stalin, and their power was far from absolute. No sinful human being can be trusted with unfettered power, as the constitutions of democratic states recognise and our knowledge of our own hearts reminds us.

The absolute sovereignty we have been considering, however, is in the hands of the God who has revealed himself in Scripture. We know that the future is shaped by his plan and, furthermore, we can be sure that his plan is perfect.

The Bible makes it clear that God's plan is an expression of his nature. In other words, God wills what he wills because of the kind of God he is. In the light of God's revelation in Scripture we can say that God's plan, his sovereign disposing of all things, is infinitely gracious, loving, and holy, just as he himself is. All the truths that we know about God that cause our hearts to rejoice are seen in his sovereign plan. What comfort that gives us!

The Lord himself provides a summary of his perfections in his revelation to Moses in Exodus 34:6, 7: 'The LORD, the LORD, a God merciful and gracious, slow to anger, and abounding in steadfast love and faithfulness, keeping steadfast love for thousands, forgiving iniquity and transgression and sin, but who will by no means clear the guilty.' Here is a list that should make the Christian's heart sing! We might also note Abraham's question to the Lord, 'Shall not the Judge of all the earth do what is just?' (Gen. 18:25), and David's assertion in Psalm 25:10, 'All the paths of the LORD are steadfast love and faithfulness.' David's language reminds us of the covenant bond between God and his people (see Lev. 26:12).

Above all, we need to remember that God's plan is carried out in and through the Lord Jesus Christ. That knowledge provides all the reassurance we need. This is the Christ who proclaimed after he was raised from the dead, 'All authority in heaven and on earth has been given to me' (Matt. 28:18). As the eternal Son he always possessed 'all authority,' but now he speaks as the incarnate Son, crucified and risen, the only Mediator. His mediatorial kingship embraces all things.

We are therefore assured that the God who holds the future is revealed perfectly in our loving and gracious Saviour. We can rest in the conviction that God's plan is perfect because it is in the hands of 'the Son of God who loved me and gave himself for me' (Gal. 2:20).

3. God is glorified in all things

We have seen that the God who holds the future is working out his eternal plan in Christ. But what is the goal of that plan? We might most readily think of how God's plan results in our salvation and the gift of eternal life. Those are wonderful thoughts that should fill us with thanksgiving, but we need to realise that God's plan is not ultimately all about us. In fact, as the Bible shows from start to finish, the goal of the plan of God is the glory of God. All that God does ultimately serves his glory.

In the broadest sense God is glorified in everything he does. Thus in Isaiah 6:3 the seraphim cry out, 'Holy, holy, holy is the LORD of hosts, the whole earth is full of his glory!' The psalmist David also proclaims, 'The heavens declare the glory of God' (Psa. 19:1). At every point in his creation God is glorified—not that his glory is increased, but it is manifested.

The entire creative work of God reveals his glory, despite the damage that human sin has wrought upon it. The earth is still the Lord's and all its fulness (Psa. 24:1), and the damage will in the end be reversed. Thus the hosts in heaven can say, 'Worthy are you, our Lord and God, to receive glory and honour and power, for you created all things, and by your will they existed and were created' (Rev. 4:11).

With reference to the salvation of sinners, Ephesians 1 takes us right to the heart of what God is doing. We are told in verses 4-6, 'In love he predestined us for adoption as sons through Jesus Christ, according to the purpose of his will, to the praise of his glorious grace, with which he has blessed us in the Beloved.' The lesson is repeated in verse 12: 'so that we who were the first to hope in Christ might be to the praise of his glory.'

The great goal of salvation is the manifestation of the glory of God in a people saved from sin and remade in the image of God, a people who will reflect his glory to the entire universe 'in the coming ages' (Eph. 2:7).

The Bible speaks of a glorious future towards which the Lord is working as he fulfils his eternal plan. In the following chapters we will be thinking about many aspects of that future which God has revealed to us. We can look forward with confidence to the new creation, when 'the earth will be filled with the knowledge of the glory of the LORD as the waters cover the sea' (Hab. 2:14).

1

Facing Death

It was the American polymath Benjamin Franklin who stated, 'in this world nothing can be said to be certain, except death and taxes.' There may be ways of avoiding taxes, but there is no way of finally avoiding death. Despite the amazing promises that are sometimes made, modern medicine, perhaps allied to new technologies, may offer extended lifespans, at least to those who can afford the costs, but at some point the result will inevitably be defeat. The process of aging and deteriorating may be slowed down a little, although that may in fact allow some late-onset diseases to develop, but sooner or later death will win. It cannot finally be avoided.

If we are to think honestly about the future, as we must do in our study of the Bible's teaching about the last things, we must reckon with the fact of death. That is the case, not only because we want our theology to be as close as possible to the truth that God has revealed in the Bible, but also because this subject has such wide-ranging pastoral implications. Virtually every aspect of how we live our lives is impacted by the inevitability of death, and every pastor has had to minister to people fearful of the approaching end of life.

Many, of course, refuse to face up to the fact of death, and modern western cultures generally do all they can to deny or conceal its realities, but death simply will not go away. It is one of the unavoidable experiences that will come to everyone. It was the German Reformer Martin Luther who observed, 'Every man must do two things alone: he must do his own believing and his own dying'.

Christians must face death just like everyone else. The experience may be difficult and painful—we should not pretend otherwise. Nevertheless, in the light of what the Bible says about those who trust in Christ as Lord and Saviour, Christians can face death in a spirit of hope—hope based on the work of a Saviour who has defeated death.

1. *Death is a sad reality*

In thinking about death in a biblical way, one very signif-icant text is Hebrews 9:27, 'it is appointed for man to die once, and after that comes judgment'. This verse is saying much more than 'Death is inevitable'. We are told 'it is appointed'.

It is common to hear death described as nothing more than the natural end of life. Death, it is claimed, is simply the normal physical pattern, driven by evolutionary forces. One day an answer to death may be found, but in the meantime it has to be accepted with as much equanimity as we can muster. Heretical groups such as the Pelagians in the early church and the Socinians in the days of the Reformation taught that Adam in the Garden of Eden was mortal and would have died regardless of his disobeying God. Many philosophers and even theologians have held that death is totally natural. Hebrews 9:27 says something profoundly different.

Notice that the verse states 'it is appointed.' Clearly implied is an element of imposition by authority. Death is not merely natural. The question is then, 'Who appoints man to die?' There can only be one answer: God appoints man to die. He alone has the authority and the power to appoint every member of the human race to die. Death should therefore be thought of in terms of God's decree as ruler of the universe, indeed of a judicial sentence imposed by the judge.

How are we to explain such language? Why does God appoint man to die? To find the explanation we must go back to the earliest history of the human race recorded in the first three chapters of the book of Genesis. The Bible itself treats these chapters as a reliable historical record (as the apostle Paul, for example, does in Romans 5).

Placed in the abundance of Eden's well-stocked garden, the commitment of Adam (and Eve) to God's authority was to be demonstrated in obedience to a single prohibition: 'of the tree of the knowledge of good and evil you shall not eat, for in the day that you eat of it you shall surely die' (Gen. 2:17). A single prohibition, yet Adam disobeyed. Adam and Eve fell for the temptation of Satan, speaking through the serpent: 'you will be like God, knowing good and evil' (Gen. 3:5). Adam and Eve wanted to replace God as the arbiter of good and evil, right and wrong. And the result of that act of disobedience was disaster for them and for the entire human race. Adam now stood before God as a guilty sinner, and the Judge's threatened sentence was imposed: 'you are dust, and to dust you shall return' (Gen. 3:19).

There are several aspects of death as described in Scripture that we must take into account.

Most obviously, there is the death of the body: 'the dust returns to the earth as it was, and the spirit returns to God who gave it' (Eccles. 12:7).

The deepest meaning of 'life,' however, is life in fellowship with God, knowing him (John 17:3), and so the deepest meaning of 'death' is separation from God, under his holy wrath. This is spiritual death, and Adam died spiritually the moment he sinned. The death of his body would follow in God's time.

The Bible shows that death is profoundly unnatural—man was not created for this experience. In Eden, as God had arranged his world, Adam represented the whole human race and so all people share in Adam's poisoned legacy: 'in Adam all die' (1 Cor. 15:22). Paul explains further in Romans 5:12, 'sin came into the world through one man, and death through sin, and so death spread to all men because all sinned.' We die because we share in the sin and guilt of Adam and are ourselves sinners. This fact explains the statement in Hebrews 9:27: 'after that comes judgment.' Surely the most fearful aspect of death is what lies beyond. There is an awareness in those who bear the image of God, however defaced by sin, that death entails a summons to sinful men and women to face a holy God. The apostle Paul in 1 Corinthians 15:56 reminds us that the sting of death is sin. Because of our fallen, sinful condition, we must all reckon seriously with the death that cannot be avoided. Death truly is the 'last enemy' (1 Cor. 15:26).

2. Death is a defeated enemy

If this was all the Bible had to say about death, it would plunge us into despair. There would be no hope for any of us. Death would usher us into the presence of a condemning judge. We can be thankful, however, that this is only part of the story. Alongside the bad news of the fact of death there is the good news of its defeat by the Lord Jesus Christ.

One glorious aspect of the saving work of Christ is set out in Hebrews 2:14, 15: 'he himself likewise partook of the same things [i.e. 'flesh and blood'], that through death he might destroy the one who has the power of death, that is, the devil, and deliver all those who through fear of death were subject to lifelong slavery.' By his death and resurrection Christ has dealt with the sin of his people and with all its consequences, including death.

We have already noted our link with Adam that results in our liability to death in all its forms. The apostle draws a striking contrast between Christ's achievement and that of Adam in Romans 5:18, 'one act of righteousness leads to justification and life for all men.' Because God 'made him to be sin who knew no sin' for our sake (2 Cor. 5:21), the full penalty, death included, is removed from all who trust in Christ. The work has been completed and the comprehensive victory has been won.

Whereas Adam was the death-bringer, Christ is the life-giver. He summed up his mission in this way: 'I came that they may have life and have it abundantly' (John 10:10). As the Good Shepherd he provided life for his sheep by laying down his own life in a substitutionary, redemptive death. He provides life in its fullest sense—'eternal life' (John 10:28)—life in fellowship with God, the life of the covenant-bond between the Lord and his people.

The Bible makes it clear that the 'life' that Christ gives to those who trust in him relates to the whole person, to their body as well as to their soul. This is the reversal of the 'death' that also relates to the whole person. Salvation delivers the body from the grave as well as the soul from hell. Ignoring or making light of the body and its needs is characteristic of Greek philosophy, not of the Bible. Jesus includes both aspects in his wonderful promise to Martha in John 11:25, 26: 'I am the resurrection and the life. Whoever believes in me, though he dies, yet shall he live, and everyone who lives and believes in me shall never die.' The crucial question is 'Do you believe this?' (verse 26).

The precious truth for the Christian is that, united to Christ in his death and resurrection, he can view death as a defeated enemy. As Paul states in 1 Corinthians 15:22, 'For as in Adam all die, so also in Christ shall all be made alive.' It is not a statement of universal salvation. Every individual will not be made alive, but all in saving union with Christ will enjoy eternal life. Without minimising the sad reality of death, Paul can speak in defiant terms: 'O death, where is your victory?' (1 Cor. 15:56), and he concludes with resounding confidence, 'But thanks be to God, who gives us the victory through our Lord Jesus Christ' (verse 57).

3. Death does not separate from God

Having considered what the Bible says about the victory of Christ over death, it is clear that for the Christian his death cannot in any sense be a satisfaction for sin. There is nothing left to pay and, as Romans 8:1 states, 'There is therefore now no condemnation for those who are in Christ Jesus.'

We cannot, however, avoid the hard fact that Christians die, and inevitably the question arises, Why does God permit his children to die physically? If Enoch and Elijah could be taken directly to heaven, why not every believer?

In general, we can say that death is one consequence of our continuing to live in a fallen world. Just as our salvation is not completed all at once, so all the effects of sin on believers, and on the creation, are not removed all at once. According to Romans 8:22-25, both creation and God's people 'groan' as they long for the consummation of salvation in complete renewal. Enduring suffering and facing the end of life should stimulate our hope of glory. In God's wisdom death will meet its final end at Christ's return: 'The last enemy to be destroyed is death' (1 Cor. 15:26).

We may therefore conclude that our passing through death must serve the Lord's purpose of conforming us to Christ and so advancing our sanctification. Indeed, facing death, and preparing for it in a godly way, is the final step in that sanctification. This is Paul's aim: 'that I may know him and the power of his resurrection, and may share his sufferings, becoming like him in his death' (Phil. 3:10). For the Christian death serves a godly, sanctifying purpose.

Of course, death in many ways entails separation—from loved ones and familiar activities—but it does not separate us from the Lord. Having surveyed all that might threaten such separation—death included—the apostle Paul concludes that nothing 'will be able to separate us from the love of God in Christ Jesus our Lord' (Rom. 8:38, 39). Indeed, death ushers us into a place of greater blessedness.

2

Beyond the Grave

Many people are fascinated by what are claimed to be accounts of the experiences of people who have gone beyond death—who died and then returned to life, and are now able to describe something of what it is like 'on the other side.' Frequently they bring back stories about bright lights, beautiful places, and radiant, gentle beings. Some are even cast in Christian terms, including meeting with Jesus, who is invariably kind and accepting.

Often these accounts of life beyond death are provided by people who were technically 'dead' for a short time, perhaps in the course of surgery or as the result of some traumatic episode. However, if these experiences are to be explained—and we do not deny that people have experienced, in many cases, something very unusual—it has to be said that none of those who had them was truly 'dead.' Some bodily functions may have stopped temporarily, but all these people soon recovered. They had not gone 'beyond death.'

The fact is that what we genuinely know about the condition of people beyond death is the information that has been revealed to us by the Lord himself. As we have noted in the previous chapter, he is sovereign over death, and so he alone is able to tell us what lies beyond.

It is significant that the Bible concentrates on the experience of believers beyond death. A very limited amount of information is provided regarding unbelievers, but enough to make it clear that to leave this life unsaved is to enter a fearful place that all should wish to avoid. We are told in 2 Peter 2:9 that 'the Lord knows how ... to keep the unrighteous under punishment until the day of judgment.' Also relevant is Jesus' parable of the Rich Man and Lazarus in Luke 16:19ff. Whatever we make of issues such as the conversation between the rich man in Hades and Abraham in heaven, one thing is clear: the rich man after death is 'in anguish in this flame' (verse 24) and cries out to Abraham for mercy. For the unsaved beyond death there is the experience of God's wrath on their sin. The only hope of avoiding such pain is the saving grace of God in Jesus Christ. It is on the state of believers beyond death that the Bible concentrates our attention.

1. *The status of believers*
First, we should recall the assurance of Romans 8:38, 39, where the apostle Paul testifies of his certainty that nothing in the entire creation, death and life included, 'will be able to separate us from the love of God in Christ Jesus our Lord.' That has implications for the believer who has died.

He or she is not separated from God's love for a moment. The most important fact about believers beyond the grave is that they are enveloped in God's eternal love.

The key phrase in Paul's statement of Romans 8 is 'in Christ Jesus our Lord.' This is language that is often encountered in Scripture. For example, we read in Revelation 14:13, 'Blessed are the dead who die *in the Lord*'—their blessedness rooted in their union with Christ. They are thus 'the dead *in Christ*' (1 Thess. 4:16). In death, as in life, believers are first and foremost 'in Christ.' Indeed, given the frequency with which he uses the term 'in Christ,' it seems to be one of Paul's favourite descriptions of a Christian.

The most fundamental truth about a Christian is his union with Christ. Everything that he is and everything that he looks forward to is based on this fact of his being in union with Christ—'in Christ.' This is how we are to understand the new status that God has granted to us.

One of the fullest biblical expositions of union with Christ is found in Romans 6. There the apostle explains that, spiritually speaking, the believer has died with Christ and has been raised to new life with Christ. Christ literally died and rose again as the representative of his people: he took their sin and its consequences, and by the grace of God they die to the old sin-dominated life and are raised to a new God-empowered life in union with Christ—'in Christ.' This is how we are to understand our status: 'our old self was crucified with him in order that the body of sin might be brought to nothing, so that we would no longer be enslaved to sin. … Now if we have died with Christ, we believe that we will also live with him' (Rom. 6:6, 8). The Saviour has been crucified and has risen for us and so, before, during, and after death, we are united to him.

Underlying the language of union with Christ is God's Covenant of Grace. The beautiful covenant relationship into which God brings his people is summed up concisely in Leviticus 26:12: 'I will walk among you and will be your God, and you shall be my people.' Notice that God does not simply give gifts to his people: he gives *himself* to them. In the full light of the New Testament we understand that he gives himself to his people in Christ and takes them to be his own in Christ. Because it depends on God's grace, the covenant cannot and will not be broken. The status of believers beyond the grave is exactly what it was in this life: covenant people in union with Christ.

2. *The location of believers*

Where are believers who have died in Christ? The Bible does not specify some geographical location. We are dealing with 'the spirits of the righteous made perfect' (Heb. 12:23) and so we are not to think in material, physical terms.

We may begin with Jesus' words to the repentant criminal in Luke 23:43, 'Truly, I say to you, today you will be with me in paradise.' Whatever the man may have expected regarding Jesus coming into his kingdom (verse 42), he would in fact experience personal fellowship with Jesus in Paradise that very day: no period of unconsciousness, no interruption to his newly established fellowship with his Saviour. We can understand why the Jehovah's Witnesses, in order to defend their belief in 'soul sleep,' translate Luke 23:43 as 'Truly, I tell you today, You will be with me in Paradise' (New World Translation), so that the telling is 'today' but the 'being' is at an unspecified future time after a period of soul-sleep. The real thrust of the text is thus removed—*unjustifiably*.

We might also note Paul's statement in Philippians 1:23, 'My desire is to depart and be with Christ, for that is far better.' The apostle's wording makes it clear that departing and being with Christ are coordinate experiences; they are two ways of looking at the same event, namely Paul's death. The departing and the being with Christ are simultaneous. Paul envisages no interval between departing from this world through death and his being with Christ in heavenly glory. There is no place for soul-sleep or for a period of unconsciousness. How could such a period of unconscious sleep be 'far better' than his present, albeit imperfect, fellowship with his Saviour? Entering into the presence of Christ is 'gain' for all believers—'to die is gain' says the apostle (verse 21), and Paul is therefore convinced that his condition after death will be 'far better.' On the basis of Paul's words we can say that when the Christian departs this life by death he is immediately with his Saviour.

Such a view is reinforced by Paul's statement in Philippians 3:2 that 'our citizenship is in heaven.' The place where Christ is presently is heaven, and that is where all who have died in him are also.

Now in heaven dwell 'the spirits of the righteous made perfect,' mentioned in Hebrews 12:23. This is the fulfilment of the promise of Christ to his disciples in John 14:3, 'that where I am you may be also.'

The beauty and warmth of the Christian's hope of life beyond the grave is made explicit in 2 Corinthians 5:1ff. The apostle Paul expresses his ultimate longing 'to put on our heavenly dwelling' (verse 2). He is speaking about the believer's resurrection body which is like the resurrected body of Christ. Until then believers will not be complete. God made us body and soul, and he saves us body and soul. Only when both body and soul are united in resurrection glory will we, as human beings made in God's image and likeness, be complete. Only then will God's work of grace have reached its goal.

Nevertheless there is great blessedness to be anticipated beyond the grave in this 'intermediate' period. And so Paul writes in verse 8, 'we would rather be away from the body and at home with the Lord.' The word 'home' is striking in its use here. All that is good and joyful about *home* is fulfilled for the Christian when he passes through death and enters the Lord's presence. It is again significant that Paul envisages no interval between the two experiences: to be away from the body is to be at home with the Lord.

Such assurances about life with the Lord beyond the grave ought to strengthen the Christian's hope –a hope that will never disappoint us—and also stir our anticipation of what lies ahead for us 'in Christ.'

3. *The activity of believers*

Beyond these facts, we are not told much about this life for God's people beyond the grave. We probably could not understand it even if we were told! There are several things that we do know, however:

Believers will be *conscious*: that is evident from their activity, such as praising God, as stated in Revelation 7:9, 10.

Believers will be *righteous*: they are 'the righteous made perfect' (Heb. 12:23).

The Bible also indicates that believers in glory are not idle. It tells us something about their activity.

(i) They 'rest from their labours' (Rev. 14:13). They experience relief from all the burdens and failures of this life; they experience satisfaction in what the Lord has done in them and through them. The Lord promised them, 'I will give you rest' (Matt. 11:28). 'Rest' is a rich biblical concept stretching all the way back to the beginning of the book of Genesis when God rested on his special day following his work of creation. It carried a sense of completeness, fulfilment. We will enter into the ultimate 'Sabbath rest for the people of God' (Heb. 4:9) in which we will enjoy God forever.

(ii) They praise. The visions of the book of Revelation depict the believers in heaven as a praising people. Note how the 'great multitude' of Revelation 7:9 joins in praise with the angelic host. The focus, of course, is entirely on the Lord. There is no sin to spoil their heartfelt praise of the gracious God to whom they owe everything.

(iii) They wait. This intermediate state is good, and even better that the state of God's people on earth, but it is not the best that God has in store for his people. There is more to be experienced and enjoyed when they are resurrected in body and placed within the renewed heavens and earth. Until that takes place they will long for the consummation and their vindication—'how long before you will judge and avenge …?' (Rev. 6:10). Greater things are still to come.

3

The Coming of the Kingdom

Jesus often mystified his contemporaries. Some of the things he said and did fitted with their ideas of what the Messiah would be like. Some of his miracles, for example, seemed to fulfil the predictions of the Old Testament prophets. Thus, in response to the doubts of John the Baptist, Jesus pointed to his miracles, such as the healing of the blind, the lame, and the deaf, foretold in Isaiah 35:5, 6 (see Luke 7:22). It could well appear that, on the basis of this evidence, the Messiah had come. On the other hand, some of the things he said and did appeared not to fit. That was especially true of his words about his death.

This conflict applied to Jesus' teaching about the kingdom of God (or the kingdom of heaven to use the phrase found in Matthew's Gospel). The language of 'kingdom' was familiar from the Old Testament Scriptures. Many of the Jews expected a Messiah who would liberate them from foreign oppression and restore their national pride. A major problem for them, however, was that Jesus taught that the kingdom had come, yet everything seemed to be going on as normal. It was most perplexing.

How were Jesus' hearers to make sense of this? And what about us two millennia later? The kingdom of God is mentioned throughout the Bible and is a central element in the preaching of Jesus as recorded in the Gospels. It is in fact a vital aspect of the Bible's teaching about the last things, and so we now turn to consider the *coming of the kingdom*.

1. What is the kingdom?

The idea of a God who reigns is deeply rooted in the Old Testament. 'The LORD is king for ever and ever' (Psa. 10:16). In some passages the 'kingdom' is clearly the kingship or royal dominion exercised by God: 'The LORD has established his throne in the heavens and his kingdom rules over all' (Psa. 103:19). The Lord reigns over all things—'a great king over all the earth' (Psa. 47:2)—and in particular over his redeemed, covenant people; he is 'the King of Jacob' (Isa. 41:21). God presently reigns, but there was also in the Old Testament a strong element of expectation. At some future date God's reign would be manifested in a glorious way for the judgment of his enemies (Isa. 2:10 ff.) and the deliverance of his people (Isa. 11:1ff.).

Against this background Jesus began his public ministry with the message, 'The kingdom of God is at hand; repent and believe in the gospel' (Mark 1:15), the reason being that, 'The time is fulfilled.'

Matthew provides us with a summary of Jesus' ministry: 'teaching in their synagogues and proclaiming the gospel of the kingdom and healing every disease and every affliction among the people' (Matt. 4:23).

We tend to think of 'kingdom' in terms of land ('realm') or people. These elements are not absent from the New Testament concept of the kingdom of God. One may, for example, 'enter the kingdom of God' (John 3:5). The main New Testament usage of 'kingdom', however, is not spatial but dynamic. The kingdom is God's reign, the exercise of his dominion, his kingship. 'Kingdom' is thus primarily something God does. He reigns as king. That is why Jesus can refer to the kingdom 'come with power' (Mark 9:1) and that is how his exorcisms show that 'the kingdom of God has come upon you' (Luke 11:20). Jesus' preaching of the kingdom is a proclamation that God reigns. The kingdom of God is dynamic.

In Scripture the kingdom of God is thoroughly centred on God: it is about what God does, not what man achieves. It is miraculous in its origin and growth and spread. Thus the parables of Mark 4 compare the kingdom to the growing of seed, over which the sower has no power. It is the power of God that brings in the kingdom, not the efforts of man. Jesus' preaching of the kingdom describes God's coming into the world to reveal his royal majesty and power and to effect his eternal plan of salvation. God the King is Deliverer and Saviour, fulfilling Isaiah 33:22: 'For the LORD is our judge; the LORD is our lawgiver; the LORD is our king; he will save us.'

The Jews rightly associated the future manifestation of the glory of God's reign with the figure of the Messiah (the

Lord's anointed king), whose coming they thought would transform the world. Jesus did indeed fulfil Old Testament hopes, but often in unexpected ways. The Messiah is clearly linked with God's kingship in the angel's message to Mary regarding the birth of Jesus: 'the Lord God will give to him the throne of his father David, and he will reign over the house of Jacob for ever, and of his kingdom there will be no end' (Luke 1:32, 33). The language of an eternal reign makes clear that this kingdom is not limited to some earthly, political state. It is the reign, the kingdom, of God.

The Messiah is also the King. In the Sermon on the Mount Jesus states the royal law for the citizens of the kingdom, with the exhortation and promise, 'seek first the kingdom of God and his righteousness, and all these things will be added to you' (Matt. 6:33). In forgiving sin (Luke 5:20) he exercises prerogatives that are royal and divine, and his divine royal authority empowers him to admit the repentant criminal into the presence of God: 'today you will be with me in Paradise' (Luke 23:43).

2. The kingdom has come

Jesus preached the arrival of the reign of God (Mark 1:15). The kingdom was present on earth and in a new way. The Jews had always believed that the Lord is King, but the newness of the presence of the kingdom preached by Jesus lay in the fact that the King himself was present in a way never previously experienced. There was the King, sharing human nature, walking among men, doing wonders and signs. This was no temporary visitation of God—a 'theophany' as it is termed—this was (and is) permanent, God 'manifested in the flesh' (1 Tim. 3:16), an 'incarnation.'

Jesus knew that the kingdom of God was present in him. It is he who exercises the reign of God. This is evident in the fact that Jesus' teaching was so thoroughly self-centred, with the focus on himself. Thus in Luke 11:20 he can say, 'if it is by the finger of God that I cast out demons, then the kingdom of God has come upon you.' Note also how in the final judgment the factor determining entry to 'the kingdom prepared for you from the foundation of the world' (Matt. 25:34) is one's attitude to Jesus (verses 35-46).

This was all very hard for the Jews, including Jesus' disciples, to accept. If the kingdom has come, where is the messianic army and the liberation of Israel? It is significant that at one point Jesus hid, 'knowing that they intended to come and make him king by force' (John 6:15). He was not that kind of king. Above all he would exercise his reign by dying to save his people: 'he must go to Jerusalem and suffer many things … and be killed' (Matt. 16:21). He was a Shepherd-King who 'lays down his life for the sheep' (John 10:11).

Although from the Old Testament perspective it seemed that the future revelation of God's reign would be one event, Jesus' teaching reveals that the kingdom in fact comes in two stages. The kingdom has come in the person of the Messianic King who provides salvation by his death and resurrection. The kingdom has already come, but not yet in its final glory. Already God's people experience the life and power of the 'age to come,' but better things lie ahead.

This was made clear when Jesus preached in the synagogue in Nazareth (Luke 4:16ff.). Jesus read from Isaiah 61, one of the prophet's great descriptions of the Messiah's work. Then, quoting verses 1, 2, Jesus described the work of the Anointed One as proclaiming the good news to the poor and liberty to the captives, along with recovery of sight for the blind and the liberating of the oppressed. This, he said, is 'the year of the Lord's favour' (Luke 4:19). Then Jesus made the revolutionary statement, 'today this Scripture has been fulfilled in your hearing' (verse 21). Already the kingdom has come, but notice how he omitted Isaiah's reference to 'the day of vengeance of our God.' That was no accidental omission. It was not yet time for the final revelation of the kingdom.

3. *The kingdom will come*

Sin still remains in the world and the King is rejected by many. This is not yet the culmination of God's saving reign. At present King Jesus reigns, with 'All authority in heaven and on earth' (Matt. 28:18). He is 'head over all things to the church' (Eph. 1:22). That is truly wonderful, but a greater day is coming. There will be a complete fulfilment of all the hopes and longings that the Lord has planted in the hearts of his people. Ahead lies 'the day of the Lord' (1 Thess. 5:2) of which the prophets so often spoke.

We are given a great promise in Acts 1:11: 'This Jesus, who was taken up from you into heaven, will come in the same way as you saw him go into heaven.' The Lord himself spoke prophetically of his glorious return when standing before the Sanhedrin: 'from now on you will see the Son of Man seated at the right hand of Power and coming on the clouds of heaven' (Matt. 26:64). The fulfilment is described, for example, by Paul in 1 Thessalonians 4: 'For the Lord himself will descend from heaven with a cry of command, with the voice of an archangel, and with the sound of the trumpet of God. And the dead in Christ will rise first. Then we who are alive, who are left, will be caught up together with them in the clouds to meet the Lord in the air' (verses 16, 17). Here is the fulfilment of the prayers of believers: 'your kingdom come' (Matt. 5:10).

This is the second and final stage of the coming of the kingdom of God. It will include the various events which we will go on to consider in a little more detail, such as the resurrection, the last judgment, the ushering in of the new creation, and the eternal blessedness of the Lord's people. As always, the King himself will be central. According to 2 Thessalonians 1:10, 'he comes on that day to be glorified in his saints, and to be marvelled at among all who have believed.' At that day he will be seen to be 'King of kings and Lord of lords' (Rev. 19:16). Every knee will bow to him and every tongue confess him to be Lord (Phil. 2:10, 11). To be 'with him for ever' will be the supreme blessing of the Lord's people (1 Thess. 4:17).

4. God's people are optimists

King Jesus said, 'I will build my church, and the gates of hell shall not prevail against it' (Matt. 16:18). That promise cannot fail, nor can the kingdom purpose of God be frustrated.

The Bible indicates that there will be evil on the earth until the last day. Both weeds and wheat will grow together until the harvest (Matt. 13:30). Nevertheless, the God who reigns will gather in a vast multitude of saved sinners 'that no one could number' (Rev. 7:9). As Jesus promised, 'people will come from east and west, and from north and south, and recline at table in the kingdom of God' (Luke 13:29). It is a prospect to fill us with hope and godly confidence as we serve the King of kings.

4

The Signs of the Times

C an we discern when Christ may be about to return to this world? Are there indicators of any kind that his second coming is near? He spoke of the future glorious consummation of the kingdom of God: have we any way of knowing if that will soon take place?

In some Christian circles there is much prophetic speculation about the 'end time' events, including study of what are thought to be 'signs' of the Lord's imminent return given to us in the Bible. Many books have been written claiming to coordinate biblical data with current events, particularly in the Middle East. The theology of Dispensationalism has been a powerful driving force for such activity. Often in reaction to these speculations, others seem almost to ignore the statements of the Bible, claiming that nobody really knows what we are to expect. What should our response be?

The phrase 'the signs of the times' occurs only in Matthew 16:3, in a rebuke directed by Jesus against the Pharisees and the Sadducees. What does Jesus mean by the 'signs,' and can this be linked in any way to the vivid language used in his 'Olivet Discourse' to his disciples, recorded in Matthew 24, Mark 13, and Luke 21? It does appear that Jesus speaks of certain events that will precede his return. How are we to understand 'the signs of the times'?

1. The nature of the signs

Matthew 16:3 reads, 'You know how to interpret the appearance of the sky, but you cannot interpret the signs of the times.' Jesus was replying to the request of the Pharisees and the Sadducees that he provide them with 'a sign from heaven,' no doubt to prove his identity. He rebukes their inability to interpret 'the signs of the times' and continues, 'An evil and adulterous generation seeks for a sign, but no sign will be given to it expect the sign of Jonah' (verse 4).

The Lord will not respond to demands to produce evidence for his identity, evidence which those hardened in unbelief will simply reject. The only 'sign' given will be the 'sign of Jonah'—resurrection after three days and three nights, as set out in Matthew 12:39-41.

Furthermore, there are already signs which his opponents are not responding to. There is abundant evidence of Jesus' identity as Messiah. This is borne out in his response to the doubt expressed by John the Baptist: 'Are you the one who is to come, or shall we look for another?' (Matt. 11:3). Jesus' reply points to his mighty works as indicators of his true identity: 'the blind receive their sight and the lame walk, lepers are cleansed and the deaf hear, and the dead are raised up, and the poor have good news preached to them' (verse 5). There, in effect, are the 'signs' of the Messiah's presence and the arrival of the kingdom of God. It is also significant that in John's Gospel the miracles of Jesus are often referred to as 'signs.' The changing of the water into wine at Cana is 'the first of his signs,' writes John (2:11).

Jesus rebukes the Pharisees and Sadducees in Matthew 16:3 because they already have, in his words and works, all the signs they need, but still they cannot interpret them correctly and they refuse the testimony that has been abundantly provided.

Thus, in the first instance, the 'signs of the times' have significance for Jesus' first hearers. They relate to what God has already done, indicating the decisive redemptive action that has taken place in and through his Son. Jesus will win the victory over sin, death, and the powers of evil by the cross and the empty tomb. History is moving towards its God-ordained climax when the salvation of God's people will be completed and the world will be judged. The signs are there for those who have the eyes of faith to discern them.

However, when we turn our attention to Jesus' sermon on the Mount of Olives (the 'Olivet Discourse'), recorded in Matthew 24, Mark 13, and Luke 21, we note that 'signs' also have a future application. Jesus has just spoken about the destruction of the temple (fulfilled in AD 70), when 'there will not be left one stone upon another that will not be thrown down' (Matt. 24:2). Some commentators have argued that the entire content of Jesus' discourse was fulfilled by events around the destruction of the temple by the Romans, but we must take into account the question of the disciples as Matthew records it. They ask, 'Tell us, when will these things be, and what will be the sign of your coming and of the close of the age?' (verse 3).

The question clearly has in view the whole span of history up to the Lord's return, however the disciples may have understood the issues involved at this point. The Lord does not correct the wording of their question in any way, and so we must conclude that his answer addresses both the destruction of the temple, along with the fall of Jerusalem, and also the entire course of events leading up to his return and the consummation of the kingdom. The two themes are interwoven in the discourse. At times it may not be entirely clear whether the destruction of the temple or the Lord's return is being described and indeed, on the analogy of the fulfilment of Old Testament prophecy, there may be more than one stage in the fulfilment of Jesus' words—one in AD 70 and a fuller, definitive one at his return.

Given that the destruction of the temple lies only some forty years in the future, it seems that much of what Jesus described could not be fitted into that short period, and even more conclusive are his specific statements regarding the consummation. Notice several types of signs (drawing on Matt. 24):

• Tragedies: 'wars and rumours of wars' (verse 6), 'nation will rise against nation, and kingdom against kingdom, and there will be famines and earthquakes in various places' (verse 7). All these are 'the beginning of the birth pains' (verse 8).

• The growth of evil: 'they will deliver you up to tribulation and put you to death, and you will be hated by all nations for my name's sake' (verse 9).

• The spread of the gospel: 'And this gospel of the kingdom will be proclaimed throughout the whole world as a testimony to all nations' (verse 14).

It is profoundly significant that the worldwide preaching of the gospel is the prelude to 'then the end will come' (verse 14). It is the end of the present world order and the consummation of the kingdom that are in view. In the same way Jesus follows his description of 'the abomination of desolation' (verse 15 ff.) with a reference to 'the coming of the Son of Man' (verse 27), then to awe-inspiring cosmic phenomena (verse 29), and then he describes the appearance of 'the sign of the Son of Man' (verse 30). At this point all 'will see the Son of Man coming on the clouds of heaven with power and great glory' (verse 30), and the angels will be sent to 'gather the elect from the four winds' (verse 31). The events in view are unmistakeably eschatological, as belonging to the 'last things.'

How are we to fit these diverse pieces together into a coherent picture? What role do the signs play in the Bible's teaching about the future?

2. *The ambiguity of the signs.*

We must not lose sight of Jesus' statement in Matthew 24:36: 'But concerning that day and hour no one knows, not even the angels of heaven, nor the Son, but the Father only.' The ignorance of the time of his return about which

Jesus speaks must refer to the human mind of the Messiah. As the eternal Son, the second person of the Trinity, his divine mind contains all knowledge: there is nothing that he does not know. Part of that knowledge has been communicated to Jesus' human mind, which by definition could not contain infinite knowledge. Thus among those things that he did not know, Jesus includes the time of his return.

In the light of such a text as Matthew 24:36 we must take care that, when we discuss the 'signs of the times,' we do not in any way suggest that any sign, or indeed all the signs taken together, can enable us to set a time or date, however imprecise, for the Saviour's return. The history of the church is littered with such futile attempts, which can only do harm, and we must not claim to be wiser than the Lord. We cannot work out the time of his return, nor even discern when that event is about to take place.

We can, in fact, take a further step and assert that the signs given in Scripture do not allow us to construct a detailed timetable of future events. Some Christians have sincerely believed that they could draw up charts of events that will fulfil prophecy. The number of schemes which have been proved wrong should serve as a warning against such efforts. Prophecy is not to be treated as a kind of 'history written in advance.' We have to remember that all the prophecies regarding Jesus' first coming were fulfilled, but often in ways that people did not expect or, sometimes, did not even want. Despite Isaiah 53, they did not look for a suffering and dying Messiah. Even John the

Baptist became perplexed by doubt. The same applies to prophecies and signs relating to the Lord's second advent. There will be many surprises, and attempts to construct a detailed chronology ought to be avoided.

When we look closely at the signs set out by Jesus in his Olivet Discourse, we see in them what we may term an ambiguity—a God-ordained, deliberate ambiguity. They do certainly reveal specific things that will take place in relation to Jesus' coming and to 'the close of the age' (Matt. 16:3), but they do not do so with such clarity that we can set dates or offer a timetable of events, except in the broadest of terms. The final judgment, for example, will follow the Lord's appearance, but detail is impossible. We can say that the signs both *reveal* and *conceal*. That is no accident: it is how the Lord has designed the signs. They reveal precisely what he wills to make known and they conceal precisely what he wills to keep hidden. They perfectly fulfil his purpose, as we would expect.

The signs of the Olivet Discourse seem to mix references to the fall of Jerusalem and the destruction of the temple with references to the Lord's return. It is not always clear to us which event is in view, and we must allow for multiple fulfilments, as with Old Testament prophecy. For example, the references to 'the abomination of desolation' (Matt. 24:15; Mark 13:14) and to 'Jerusalem surrounded by armies' (Luke 21:20) seem to depict the Roman siege of the city. But is that the only fulfilment? Commentators equally committed to the authority of Scripture are divided in their opinions on this matter.

We also have to take into account the fact that some of these signs occur throughout history—wars, famines, persecution, and the spread of the gospel, for example. The question then arises: how can we know whether this war or that famine is an immediate precursor of the Lord's return? The simple answer is that we cannot know. There is always going to be a high degree of uncertainty.

None of this rules out the possibility of an intensification of the events the Lord describes in his discourse. He speaks, for example, of 'such tribulation as has not been from the beginning of the creation that God created until now, and never will be' (Mark 13:19). And yet, however intense the persecution, God's people can never be sure the consummation is at hand. This ambiguity means that we must never sit back and take it easy, or tell ourselves that the Lord cannot be coming back just yet. The signs serve practical spiritual purposes, to which we will return at the end of the chapter.

We turn now to consider in a little more detail two of the main groups of signs—the growth of evil and the spread of the gospel.

3. The growth of evil

Many of the signs of which Jesus speaks in the Olivet Discourse indicate that times of great hardship lie ahead for his church. It appears that as history unfolds and the return of the Lord draws near there will be a great growth of evil.

We may perhaps draw a parallel with the tremendous upsurge in demonic activity that was evident at the first coming of the Messiah. The hosts of evil recognised their deadly enemy and reacted with (ultimately futile) violence. When the Lord returns he will exercise final judgment on his defeated enemies, and their hatred against him and his will be stirred up.

We can probably link this growth of evil to the statement of Revelation 20:7, 'And when the thousand years are ended, Satan will be released from his prison.' However precisely we understand the thousand-year imprisonment, it appears that the divine restraint on Satan currently in place will be eased and he will be permitted greater scope for his activity. In addition to deceiving the nations (verse 8), we expect him to do all he can to hinder the redemptive purpose of God. All his activity, however, remains under the Lord's sovereign control. Events are never outside God's control, however they may seem to us, and that is a truth full of comfort for the Lord's people.

(i) *Tribulation*. In the providence of God, it has always been the lot of his people to suffer persecution. It is therefore not at all surprising that among the signs about which Jesus speaks in his Olivet Discourse the violence suffered by his people is one of the most prominent. Because Jesus is addressing the disciples' two questions, regarding the destruction of the temple and his return at the 'close of the age,' aspects of both events are interwoven, as if they all took place at the same time. This is sometimes termed 'prophetic foreshortening,' when events separated by a period of time are described as if simultaneous. The Old Testament prophets often described the first and second advents of the Messiah as if they were a single event. We should also note that Jesus depicts the events around his return with the language and imagery of the world of his day, in terms of life in first-century Judea, even when they had worldwide significance. That was also characteristic of the Old Testament prophets.

'Tribulation' (Matt. 24:9) characterises the experience of God's people throughout the period between the two advents of the Lord. In John 15:20 Jesus warned his disciples (and us), 'If they persecuted me, they will also persecute you,' and in John 16:33 he stated, 'In the world you will have tribulation.' He followed the second warning, however, with the exhortation, 'But take heart, I have overcome the world'; and among the Beatitudes of the Sermon on the Mount we find, 'Blessed are those who are persecuted for righteousness' sake, for theirs is the kingdom of heaven. Blessed are you when others revile you and persecute you and utter all kinds of evil against you falsely on my account. Rejoice and be glad, for your reward is great in heaven, for so they persecuted the prophets who were before you' (Matt. 5:10-12). Tribulation tries to overwhelm believers but God's grace will uphold them. Enduring tribulation is an aspect of union with Christ as we share in suffering for his sake.

It does appear, however, that the Lord envisages an unprecedented level of tribulation at the close of the age and as his return approaches. He warns in Matthew 24:21, 'there will be great tribulation, such as has not been from the beginning of the world until now, and never will be.'

That the ultimate fulfilment of his warning is related to the last things is evident from verse 29ff. He begins with the statement, 'Immediately after the tribulation of those days the sun will be darkened, and the moon will not give its light, and the stars will fall from heaven, and the powers of the heavens will be shaken' (verse 29). Most significantly, these cosmic upheavals will be followed by 'the Son of Man coming on the clouds of heaven with power and great glory' (verse 31), the prelude to the last judgment (verse 31).

It seems that the sign of tribulation characterises the whole period between the Lord's first and second advents, with an intensification towards the end. The ambiguity remains: we cannot say definitively that a particular experience of tribulation is the final one. That is the pattern for each sign.

(ii) *Apostasy.* Perhaps bound up with the persecution that the church experiences is a warning of significant apostasy from the faith: 'And then many will fall away and betray one another and hate one another' (Matt. 24:10). In the context of this apostasy false prophets and false christs are also mentioned (verses 11, 24). The cost of genuine discipleship is too high for many. That is not to suggest that true believers can finally fall: it always remains the case that 'they will never perish and no one will snatch them out of my hand' (John 10:28). The falsity of the profession of many will, however, be exposed.

Episodes of apostasy have occurred among the professing people of God throughout history, but again it does seem that we are to expect an intensification of this as the end approaches. Thus Paul warns, 'Now the Spirit expressly says that in later times some will depart from the faith by devoting themselves to deceitful spirits and teachings of demons' (1 Tim. 4:1). More explicit are his comments in 2 Thessalonians 2:1, 3: 'Now concerning the coming of our Lord Jesus Christ and our being gathered together to him … that day will not come unless the rebellion comes first.' The word translated 'rebellion' is in fact 'apostasy.' It appears that at the end of the present age there will be a significant falling away from (apparent) Christian commitment, such that the false and the genuine will be more clearly separated. Again, the inbuilt ambiguity of the sign means that we cannot point with certainty to a particular falling away as 'the apostasy' of 2 Thessalonians 2.

(iii) *Antichrist*. Some Christians are fascinated by the figure of the Antichrist and numerous theories about the figure's identity have come and gone. The scarcity of biblical material means that we should not give this issue inflated significance. We must try to keep within biblical bounds.

In 2 Thessalonians 2:3 Paul indicates that, together with the apostasy, 'the day of the Lord' (verse 2) will not come unless 'the man of lawlessness is revealed, the son of destruction.' The reference to taking his seat 'in the temple of God' suggests something that takes place within the institution of the church. Bearing in mind that in Greek 'anti' can mean 'in place of,' as well as 'against,' it seems that the figure presents himself as a counterfeit god: 'opposes and exalts himself against every so-called god or object of worship … proclaiming himself to be God' (verse 4).

Jesus warns that 'many false prophets will arise and lead many astray' (Matt. 24:11). This has been characteristic of the whole period between his first and second advent, but again it seems that this will intensify towards the end, leading to 'the man of lawlessness.'

We may link this with the reference to 'the antichrist' in 1 John. In 1 John 2:22 we read, 'This is the antichrist, he who denies the Father and the Son.' In verse 18 John states that 'now many antichrists have come. Therefore we know that it is the last hour.' The spirit of Antichrist was already at work in John's day.

Who or what is the Antichrist? Both personal and institutional identifications have been made. The Reformers and the Westminster Divines saw the Pope in these verses. That may well be an element in understanding the description, but a more precise identification is probably not possible. Most important is the Lord's destruction of Antichrist 'with the breath of his mouth' (2 Thess. 2:8). He does not merit undue attention.

4. The spread of the gospel

As evil grows in influence, so too the gospel will spread powerfully throughout the world. There is a great missionary promise in Matthew 24:14: 'this gospel of the kingdom will be proclaimed throughout the whole world as a testimony to all nations, and then the end will come.' Before the return of Christ the gospel will be preached to the ends of the earth.

What will the result be? Though there will always be those who reject the gospel, God's word will always be fruitful and will 'accomplish that which I purpose' (Isa. 55:11). Note Psalm 67:7 as but one example: 'God blesses us, that all the ends of the earth may fear him' (NASB). This worldwide proclamation of the gospel will bring in many of the 'great multitude that no one could number' (Rev. 7:9). Every nation and people-group will be represented. The implications for the Jewish people will be considered in the next chapter.

Only the Lord will know when the testimony has reached 'all nations,' but we have the absolute certainty that his glorious redeeming work will be embraced by every one of the elect, and so we truly are gospel optimists.

5. *The call of the signs*

As was the case with the Pharisees and Sadducees, the signs of the times summon the unsaved to repentance. A testimony to the Messiah is available for all with eyes willing to see and ears willing to hear. With regard to Christians the signs should cultivate a certain mindset:

(i) *Watchfulness.* 'Therefore, stay awake, for you do not know on what day your Lord is coming' (Matt. 4:42). We must remain spiritually alert, using the means of grace and battling sin. There is no room for complacency or carelessness.

(ii) *Service.* Every Christian is to be a 'faithful and wise servant' (Matt. 24:45), using his gifts and opportunities to serve the Lord. 'Blessed is that servant whom his master will find so doing when he comes' (verse 46).

(iii) *Hopefulness.* Although there may be many issues relating to the Lord's return about which we are uncertain, Christians are people of 'hope' in the biblical sense of 'certainty.' All things are in the hands of our sovereign God and he will work out every detail of his plan for his glory and our salvation.

5

The Future of the Jewish People

W hen faith and politics meet, they can produce a very powerful mixture. For many Christians that is particularly the case in relation to the State of Israel. Many believe that they should offer whatever support they can to the nation that was set up as a Jewish homeland because, in their view, this has happened in fulfilment of Old Testament prophecy. In the United States in particular, certain political policies are promoted because of an acceptance of this view of prophecy, and to some Christians it is inconceivable that there could be any other understanding of what Scripture says about 'Israel.' There is inevitably also much interest in the future of Israel and its impact on surrounding nations.

As we turn to consider the future of the Jewish people, our aim will be to stay as close to the biblical witness as possible and to avoid any speculation that is not grounded in the word of God. Our search must be for what God has revealed about this important matter.

1. *Laying the foundations*

We need to begin by establishing certain biblical principles relating to the Jewish people which will guide our thinking on the subject. We need to be clear particularly about the role of Jesus the Messiah and about the place of Jews and Gentiles in the people of God.

(i) *Jewish identity*. In Romans 9 the apostle Paul is wrestling with questions regarding the general Jewish rejection of Jesus Christ and of the gospel. He writes in verse 6, 'But it is not as though the word of God has failed. For not all who are descended from Israel belong to Israel.' The apostle goes on to stress that the crucial issue is not physical descent from Abraham: 'not all are children of Abraham because they are his offspring' (verse 7). God's promise was to bless those descended from Abraham only through Isaac, the son of promise. Consequently, 'This means that it is not the children of the flesh who are children of God, but the children of the promise are counted as offspring' (verse 8).

A passage like this indicates that the Bible is less concerned with ethnicity and much more with spirituality. Paul spells this out in Romans 2:28, 29, 'for no one is a Jew who is merely one outwardly, nor is circumcision outward and physical. But a Jew is one inwardly, and circumcision is a matter of the heart, by the Spirit, not by the letter.' Thus circumcision is fundamentally not an ethnic sign but a spiritual sign. In Abraham's case it was 'a seal of the righteousness that he had by faith while he was still uncircumcised' (Rom. 4:11). It is therefore crucial for us to 'walk in the footsteps of the faith that our father

Abraham had before he was circumcised' (verse 12). That faith is in the coming Messiah, Jesus, and in Galatians 3:29 Paul makes the powerful statement regarding all believers: 'if you are Christ's, then you are Abraham's offspring, heirs according to promise.'

The fulfilment of true Jewish identity comes through the faith in Christ which brings the justification which Abraham experienced, together with all the blessings of salvation. Thus the prophets, by the ministry of the Holy Spirit, spoke of 'the sufferings of Christ and the subsequent glories' (1 Pet. 1:11). Faith in Messiah Jesus is at the centre of true Jewishness.

It must be stressed that nothing in Scripture provides the slightest justification for anti-Semitism in thought, word, or action. It is a vile sin, and it is also tragic that in the course of history it has been committed by those who claimed the name of Christ. The God-honouring Christian attitude to the Jewish people is a love which longs for their salvation through faith in Jesus Christ.

(ii) *The land*. What is the significance of the 'land,' so precious to Jewish people? The land of Canaan was given to Abraham as one of the blessings of the Lord's covenant with him: 'I will give to you and to your offspring after you the land of your sojournings, all the land of Canaan, for an everlasting possession, and I will be their God' (Gen. 17:8). This is of course taken by many as a warrant for the present-day state of Israel.

We must, however, take into account the faith of the patriarchs and their descendants in the Messiah to come.

In Hebrews 11:13 we read that the patriarchs 'died in faith, not having received the things promised, but having seen them and greeted them from afar, and having acknowledged that they were strangers and exiles on the earth.' As the writer then states, 'people who speak thus make it clear that they are seeking a homeland' (verse 14), and it is further specified that 'they desire a better country, that is, a heavenly one' (verse 16). The fulfilment is then made clear: 'Therefore God is not ashamed to be called their God, for he has prepared for them a city.'

In the light of these passages we can say that the hope of the patriarchs was not ultimately for some square miles of territory in Canaan—it was for a heavenly city, the goal of their faith in the coming Messiah. As Paul shows in Galatians 3:16, the offspring (or 'seed') of Abraham through whom the promised inheritance is realised 'is Christ.' The physical, earthly 'land' was thus a token and foreshadowing of the rich covenant blessings that all believers receive in Christ. God so decreed events 'that the promise by faith in Jesus Christ might be given to those who believe' (verse 22). The land of Canaan was a temporal, material picture of the riches given in Christ, which will culminate in the glories of the new creation—'new heavens and a new earth in which righteousness dwells' (2 Pet. 3:13).

The present secular state of Israel does not offer a fulfilment of prophecy. Christian attitudes to it must be shaped by biblical principles of justice, security, and compassion that embrace both Jews and Palestinians. The long history of conflict indicates how great that challenge is.

(iii) *One people*. As noted above, the Abrahamic covenant promises are fulfilled in Christ to all who believe (Gal. 3:29). Thus the promises include all believers, both Jews and Gentiles. There is only one people of God—and always has been—those redeemed by the blood of Messiah Jesus. It is vital to see that in Romans 11:17ff. Paul describes the people of God as a single olive tree, from which some Jewish branches have been broken off and to which Gentile branches have been engrafted. There are not two trees, but one. Together in Christ, believing Jews and believing Gentiles are expressions of God's single saving purpose. The church does not 'replace' Israel, as some would have it. By God's grace Israel has grown into and found fulfilment in the church drawn from all nations. The church must never forget it is grafted into the olive tree of Israel.

2. Describing the people

(i) *A privileged people*. God granted to the Jewish people great blessings and privileges: 'to them belong the adoption, the glory, the covenants, the giving of the law, the worship, and the promises,' culminating in the fact that 'from their race, according to the flesh, is the Christ, who is God over all, blessed for ever' (Rom. 9:4, 5). It is a wonderful list of blessings and privileges, all testimonies to God's love and grace.

Rightly, they look back with reverence to Abraham, to the covenant God made with him and his descendants, and to the promises which he was given. As Galatians 3:8 states, 'the Scripture, foreseeing that God would justify the

Gentiles by faith, preached the gospel beforehand to Abraham, saying, "In you shall all the nations be blessed."' In the Abrahamic covenant the Jewish people had the gospel of the Messiah's redeeming work, the message that pointed them to the Lamb that God would provide as a substitute for sinners, just as he provided the ram for Abraham to sacrifice instead of his son Isaac on Mount Moriah (Gen. 22). The whole system of sin offerings commanded in the law of Moses proclaimed the same truth.

Such privileges of course bring great responsibilities. The promises of the covenant had to be received in faith, since 'it is those of faith who are the sons of Abraham' (Gal. 3:7).

(ii) *A needy people*. We have already noted the statement of Romans 9:6, 'not all who are descended from Israel belong to Israel.' Many did not receive the covenant promises in faith—a great grief to Paul's heart—and so 'some of the branches [of the olive tree] were broken off' (Rom. 11:17).

The heart of the problem is set out in Romans 9:31, 32. 'Israel, who pursued a law that would lead to righteousness, did not succeed in reaching that law. Why? Because they did not pursue it by faith, but as if it were based on works.' In practice they sought 'to establish their own righteousness' (Rom. 10:3). They rejected the grace available in Messiah Jesus and sought to earn divine favour, as many Jews do today.

Thus Jewish people need the gospel, just as Gentiles do. It is not anti-Semitic to point Jews to Jesus the Messiah, whose blood alone can save them. It is to him that they are directed by their Scriptures. Love requires the sharing of the gospel with them. Whether Jew or Gentile, 'everyone who calls on the name of the Lord will be saved' (Rom. 10:13).

(iii) *A blessed people.* Despite the present 'cutting off' of so many Jewish branches, chapters 9–11 of Romans leads us to believe that God has a glorious spiritual future for the Jewish people. Even now there is 'a remnant, chosen by grace' (10:5): a growing remnant, but greater things are still to come.

In these key chapters the apostle Paul makes several crucial points. In chapter 9 he argues that God's rejection of Israel is not complete: out of ethnic Israel he has always been calling his elect to faith and salvation in Jesus. In chapter 10 he affirms that God's rejection is not arbitrary. Jews are responsible for their actions: 'they did not submit to God's righteousness' (10:3). In chapter 11 he asserts that God's rejection is neither absolute nor unqualified: there is a great hope for the Jews.

At present 'salvation has come to the Gentiles, so as to make Israel jealous' (11:11). The bringing in of the Gentiles is God's amazing way of provoking Jews to spiritual jealousy and thus bringing them to saving faith in Jesus. In his own time God will move in power and grace to bring many Jews to faith in Christ. Listen to Paul's joy: 'Now if their trespass means riches for the world, and if their failure means riches for the Gentiles, how much more will their full inclusion [lit. 'their fulness'] mean?' (11:12).

Jewish branches can and will be grafted back in to the one olive tree: 'even they, if they do not continue in their unbelief, will be grafted in, for God has the power to graft them in again' (11:23). This is how God is at work: 'a partial hardening has come upon Israel, until the fulness of the Gentiles has come in. And in this way all Israel will be saved' (11:25, 26).

Who is 'all Israel'? In every other case in these chapters 'Israel' is an ethnic designation—Jews—and so must be here too. The full number of elect Jews will be brought in by God's amazing grace: 'as regards election, they are beloved for the sake of their forefathers. For the gifts and calling of God are irrevocable' (11:28, 29).

As another 'sign of the times,' therefore, we may look for many conversions among Jewish people.

6

The Promised Return of Christ

In constructing a systematic summary of biblical truth—a 'systematic theology'—we must be careful to reflect the priorities and emphases of the Bible. If we do not approach the task in that way, we risk giving undue prominence to subjects about which the Bible has little to say, but which we find fascinating or even exciting, whilst at the same time relegating to the background matters which are of great importance and about which the Bible has a lot to say. The resulting 'theology' is liable to reflect our quirks and prejudices, rather than God's priorities.

Eschatology (the doctrine of the last things) is one part of theology where such risks are significant. It is easy to become wrapped up in speculation about, for example, 'the rapture,' which does not figure largely in the New Testament, and which we will consider in a later chapter, whilst at the same time skimming quickly over matters that are central to the last things. In particular we need always to keep at the front of our minds that at the heart of biblical revelation regarding eschatology is the promised return of the Lord Jesus Christ in grace and judgment. That glorious event must not be treated superficially or moved from its central position. Biblical eschatology is about the 'second coming' of the Lord. Christians may disagree on some matters relating to the last things, but regarding the central fact of the Lord's return there should be complete agreement.

As he prepared his disciples for his approaching death in his discourse in the Upper Room, Jesus promised, 'if I go and prepare a place for you, I will come again and take you to myself, that where I am you may be also' (John 14:3). Whilst it might be argued that this 'coming again' is with reference to a believer's death, we have to say that the depiction of death as the Lord coming back for one of his people does not occur anywhere else in the New Testament. This promise of Jesus appears to have in view his return in glory at the last day. In the fullest sense he will then take believers to be with him.

Whatever our view of John 14:3, Jesus provides a clear reference to his return in his powerful words to the high priests and the Sanhedrin when standing trial before them: 'I tell you, from now on you will see the Son of Man seated at the right hand of Power and coming on the clouds of heaven' (Matt. 26:64). The authorities recognise this as a claim to deity and accuse Jesus of blasphemy, but it is a direct assertion that, at God's appointed time, he will return in the glory of deity.

What emerges from Jesus' teaching, in harmony with the rest of the New Testament, is that the dying Saviour will not only rise from the dead, but will come again. The return of Christ is central to Christian hope, and several characteristics of that promised return may be noted.

1. Certain

When we considered the coming of the kingdom as taught by Jesus, we saw that 'already' the kingdom has come in the person of King Jesus, but it has 'not yet' come in its glorious fulness. The completion of the kingdom's coming awaits his return. At Jesus' ascension the angel announced, 'This Jesus, who was taken up from you into heaven, will come in the same way as you saw him go into heaven' (Acts 1:11). His return is certain. We may identify two main reasons for this certainty:

(i) *The sovereignty of God.* We are assured in Ephesians 1:11 that God is the one 'who works all things according to the counsel of his will.' Thus the plan and decree of the triune God to bring the full number of the elect into the kingdom will be fulfilled and the consummation of the kingdom in the glorious revelation of the King will certainly take place. The Son will complete the salvation of his people and also the judgment of those who continue in rebellion against God's rule.

(ii) *The victory of Christ.* Having made atonement for sin and having risen in triumph, the Saviour now reigns at the Father's right hand: 'Christ Jesus is the one who died—more than that, who was raised—who is at the right hand of God' (Rom. 8:34). That victory is now seen only with the eyes of faith; sinners are permitted to rebel; and 'he must reign until he has put all his enemies under his feet' (1 Cor. 15:25). The day must come when every knee will bow and every tongue confess his Lordship (Phil. 2:10). His victory will be consummated at his return, when all rebels will be subdued.

2. *Personal*

'This Jesus' (Acts 1:11) is the one who will return. It is the incarnate Son, the crucified and risen Messiah, the exalted King who will return personally to complete his redemptive work. The kingdom will not be consummated by a distant King but by one who has returned in glory to the place of his first coming in humility.

The final events in the history of the present world—or the world in its present form—will not be determined by human activity or by impersonal forces, but by the mighty, sovereign acts of the Lord himself. Just as each stage of human history is in the Lord's hands, so will its end be. That is a truth that is full of comfort for believers as they serve the King in a world full of uncertainty, where the Lord's people are often called to suffer for his sake. The King is coming.

As we noted in John 14:3, Jesus promised, 'I will come again.' This is in harmony with his statement in the Olivet Discourse that after the appearance of 'the sign of the Son of Man' in heaven, 'they will see the Son of Man coming in the clouds of heaven with power and great glory' (Matt. 24:30), the fulfilment of the apostle Peter's statement that God will 'send the Christ appointed for you, Jesus, whom heaven must receive until the time for restoring all things' (Acts 3:20, 21).

The focus of Christian hope is the personal return of the Saviour: 'our citizenship is in heaven,' writes Paul, 'and from it we await a Saviour, the Lord Jesus Christ' (Phil. 3:20). As we will see in a later chapter, our final glory is bound up with this event: 'When Christ who is your life appears, then you also will appear with him in glory' (Col. 3:4).

3. Visible

Nowhere does the Bible suggest that the return of Christ will be invisible (or taking place in 1914, as falsely predicted by the Jehovah's Witnesses!), or visible only to a limited number of people (in 'the rapture,' according to Dispensationalists). In Acts 1:11 we are told that Jesus 'will come in the same way as you saw him go into heaven.' He ascended visibly until a cloud hid him; consequently he will return visibly.

We have already quoted Jesus' words to the high priests at his trial, and they are most relevant to this subject of the visibility of his return: 'you will see the Son of Man seated at the right hand of Power and coming on the clouds of heaven' (Matt. 26:64). Only a visible return could fulfil that prophecy.

We should link this with Jesus' warning in the Olivet Discourse against thinking that the Son of Man on his return will go unnoticed by many. Jesus says, 'So, if they say to you, "Look, he is in the wilderness," do not go out. If they say, "Look, he is in the inner rooms," do not believe it. For as the lightning comes from the east and shines as far as the west, so will be the coming of Son of Man' (Matt. 24:26, 27). No one will be in any doubt when this event of his personal, visible return takes place.

There is a significant parallel between the first and second coming of the Lord. The first was visible and so the second will be visible. As Paul states in Titus 2, using the same word, 'the grace of God has *appeared*, bringing salvation … waiting for our blessed hope, the *appearing* of the glory of our great God and Saviour Jesus Christ' (verses 11, 13). How God will make it possible that 'every eye will see him' (Rev. 1:7) need not concern us.

4. *Glorious*

The first coming of the King was in obscurity and humility: 'he had no form or majesty that we should look at him, and no beauty that we should desire him' (Isa. 53:2). The Gospel records testify to the fulfilment of that prophecy. Although the Messiah was walking among them, many people did not recognise him, his own siblings included. 'He came to his own,' writes John, 'and his own people did not receive him' (John 1:11). Indeed, his fellow-countrymen rejected him and demanded his crucifixion by the Roman authorities.

This coming in humility indicates the nature of his redemptive mission. He did not come with a glory which would have overwhelmed people, compelling a response. He came to serve, suffer, and die for the benefit of others. He came as a servant—the Suffering Servant of Old Testament prophecies such as Isaiah 53—and so humility and obscurity were necessary. Philippians 2:7 puts it this way: he 'made himself nothing, taking the form of a servant, being born in the likeness of men.'

Without compromising his full deity, the Son of God's glory was veiled during his earthly ministry. A brief glimpse of that glory was given to three of his disciples at the transfiguration (Matt. 17:1-8; Mark 9:1-13; Luke 9:28-36), but at his second coming the veil will be removed and he will be seen 'coming on the clouds of heaven with power and great glory' (Matt. 24:30). He will appear in his full radiance as 'King of kings and Lord of lords' (Rev. 19:16), the victorious, conquering sovereign before whom all will bow, whether willingly by divine grace or unwillingly by divine power.

It is wonderful to know that believers will share in that glory: 'when he appears, we shall be like him, because we shall see him as he is' (1 John 3:2); 'When Christ, who is your life, appears, then you also will appear with him in glory' (Col. 3:4). The final stage of our salvation requires the Lord's return in glory.

5. Fearful

As we shall see in more detail a little later, for believers saved by grace, the return of King Jesus will be a day of joy and thanksgiving, but it will not be so for others.

According to Revelation 1:7, 'every eye will see him, even those who pierced him, and all tribes of the earth will wail on account of him.' How could we begin to imagine what it will be like for those who have rejected Christ to stand before him in all his glory? Those who remain in their sin, having rejected the offer of salvation in this life, will endure the full penalty their sin deserves. Paul refers to the day 'when the Lord Jesus is revealed from heaven with his mighty angels in flaming fire, inflicting vengeance on those who do not know God and on those who do not obey the gospel of our Lord Jesus' (2 Thess. 1:7, 8). To be able to look forward to and welcome the return of Christ, we must repent and believe while we have opportunity, in this the day of God's grace and favour (2 Cor. 6:2).

7

Our Resurrection Hope

Death is the ultimate challenge to any religion, worldview, or philosophy. What does it have to offer when you stand beside a grave—of a newborn who lived a few hours, of an elderly person who reached a hundred, of one who died after years of struggle with illness, or one who left this life in a moment, without warning? If the beliefs you hold and live by have no word of hope in the face of death, they are really worth little or nothing.

Christians die, just as every human being does. Having faith in Christ does not spare believers from the hard experiences of life, and the Lord never promised that it would. Unless the Lord were to return first, Christians will be called to experience death in one of its many forms. Death is something that we must reckon with—for ourselves, for our loved ones, for our fellow believers.

Writing in 1 Corinthians 15:19, the apostle Paul makes this striking statement: 'If in this life only we have hope in Christ, we are of all people most to be pitied.' If Christians have staked everything on Christ and have lived a life characterised in many ways by self-denial, then if death is really the end and the grave truly has the last word, we would have to conclude, 'What a waste!'

But death is not the end. In the first two chapters of our study we began to see how that is the case, but there is so much more to be said. It is profoundly significant that Paul, having spoken of the emptiness of a purely 'this-worldly hope,' goes on to write, 'But in fact Christ has been raised from the dead, the firstfruits of those who have fallen asleep. For as by a man came death, by a man has come also the resurrection of the dead' (1 Cor. 15:20, 21). Paul portrays Christian hope in terms of bodily resurrection—not merely the survival of the soul—and that resurrection is bound up with the return of Christ.

1. God saves the body

It was characteristic of much Greek philosophy to devalue that which was physical, whether lifeless matter or the human body. The spiritual and the divine were counted as truly valuable, whilst the material and earthly was written off as inferior, even harmful to man's spiritual flourishing. For some this was summed up in the phrase, 'The body is a tomb.' The material body was something to be escaped from and left behind. At times this wrongly influenced some Christian thinkers and teachers to ignore man's physical constitution, and even to despise the body.

However, the biblical worldview says something completely different. As chapters 1–2 of the book of Genesis show, God is the Creator of all things, including the material. Therefore the physical world (including the bodies of human beings), is not the work of an inferior creator, as some of the Greeks imagined. The Creator's final verdict on all his handiwork is of great importance for our theology: 'And God saw everything that he had made, and behold, it was *very good*' (Gen. 1:31). Nowhere in the entire creation was there anything substandard or imperfect.

The Creator's verdict clearly includes man. Uniquely, human beings were made from 'dust from the ground' into which God breathed 'the breath of life' (Gen. 2:7). The entire Bible bears witness to man's constitution as both material and spiritual, consisting of a material body and a spiritual component, variously designated 'spirit' and 'soul' (terms which are essentially synonymous). Although the spirit may continue to exist apart from the body, as it does after the body dies, God made man to be a unity of the physical and the spiritual. That is his natural state, as we see in Eden.

It is also crucial to note that the entirety of human nature has been affected by sin. Not only has sin corrupted the human spirit, it has also brought ruin to the body. The 'death' threatened by God should Adam eat of the tree of the knowledge of good and evil (Gen. 2:17) embraced all aspects of his nature and continues to impact every one of his descendants. Sin is not confined to one aspect of human nature, but corrupts it in its entirety. Consequently, when God pronounces his sentence on Adam, the body shares in the consequences of sin: 'By the sweat of your face you shall eat bread, till you return to the ground, for out of it you were taken; for you are dust, and to dust you shall return' (Gen. 3:19).

If sin embraces all of human nature, so does God's remedy for sin. Salvation is designed to save the whole man, not just one part of his constitution. The redeeming work of Christ relates to the entire being of his people. Thus when the angel tells Joseph about the birth of Jesus, he is told, 'you shall call his name JESUS, for he will save his people from their sins' (Matt. 1:21). He does not save part of them—their souls—and abandon their bodies. It could be said that Satan would have won a measure of victory had God not included man's body in salvation, but had allowed it ultimately to be lost and destroyed.

God saves people, not just souls. It has become common among Christians to speak about 'saving souls,' and appeal can be made to 1 Peter 1:9, 'obtaining the outcome of your faith, the salvation of your souls.' But we must carefully guard against any idea of salvation only including the spiritual part of man's being.

The Scriptures emphasise the comprehensive nature of the sanctification that salvation entails. In 1 Corinthians 7:34, for example, we read that 'the unmarried or betrothed woman is anxious about the things of the Lord, how to be holy in *body and spirit*.' In 2 Corinthians 7:1 we read, 'Since we have these promises, beloved, let us cleanse ourselves from every defilement of *body and spirit*, bringing holiness to completion in the fear of God.'

The body is not to be overlooked or devalued in salvation. God gives value to the body in creation and in re-creation. In Christ God saves our bodies. That is one of the reasons why the body is to be treated with great respect and why the goal of Christian hope includes the resurrection of the body.

2. Disembodiment is not the end

As we noted in a previous chapter, the Christian has the certainty of being with the Lord immediately upon death. As Paul puts it in 2 Corinthians 5:8, we will be 'away from the body and at home with the Lord.' That is a joyful prospect for us who belong to the Lord!

That disembodied state, however, is not the end as far as the blessedness of believers is concerned, and it is not the best that the Lord has prepared for us. In 2 Corinthians 5:2 Paul speaks of believers 'longing to put on our heavenly dwelling.' It seems best to understand this as a reference to our resurrection body in all its glory, with which we will be 'further clothed' (verse 4). In faith we look forward to that great event.

As Paul puts it in 2 Corinthians 5:4, the Christian's longing is 'not that we would be unclothed, but that we would be further clothed,' so that 'we may not be found naked' (verse 3). However great the joys of the disembodied life with the Lord in heaven—and there will be many of them—there is a certain unnaturalness about it. God did not create us to be like that. We were created body and soul, to be a unity. The Bible therefore portrays the believer's life immediately following the death of the body as a time of incompleteness, a time of waiting for something more and better in God's purposes of grace and salvation.

3. *We will be raised with Christ*

At the heart of the Christian's resurrection hope is his union with Christ, the fundamental truth underlying every aspect of salvation. This is the union effected by the Lord in the Covenant of Grace whereby he gives himself to us as our God and takes us as his people (see Lev. 26:12). This underlies Paul's statement in 1 Corinthians 15:22, 'For as in Adam all die, so also in Christ shall all be made alive.'

This union is crucial to resurrection: 'For if we have been united with him in a death like his, we shall certainly be united with him in a resurrection like his' (Rom. 6:5). Because we are united to Christ by grace, we die to the old life of sin and we rise to a new life of holiness. We begin to experience that new life already, and we look forward to the fulness and consummation of the new life in the resurrection of the body when Christ returns.

The fact that our unbreakable union with Christ provides for this resurrection teaches us that it is impossible for it not to take place; otherwise God's promise of salvation would have failed. What an encouragement for us as the people of God, especially in times of doubt and struggle with trials.

Note how the risen Christ is described in 1 Corinthians 15:20: 'Christ has been raised from the dead, the firstfruits of those who have fallen asleep.' Drawing on the language of the Old Testament regulations regarding the offerings to be made at the beginning of harvest, the risen Christ is described as the first part of the harvest that guarantees the gathering in of the whole crop. The implication is stated in verse 23, 'but each in his own order: Christ the firstfruits, then at his coming those who belong to Christ.' Because he is risen, never to die again, all those united to him will rise with him. As he said to his disciples, 'Because I live, you also will live' (John 14:19).

We find the same idea expressed in Colossians 1:18, where Christ is described as 'the firstborn from the dead.' He has risen and has left the realm of the dead, never to return, having won the victory over death. Not only is he the first to rise in this victorious way (others such as Lazarus would die again), he is also the cause of the resurrection of his people, those who are united to him in his death and resurrection. Again we have a clear assertion of the certainty of the resurrection of all those united to 'the firstborn.'

The Lord himself sets out our great resurrection hope in addressing the crowd in John 6:40: 'For this is the will of my Father, that everyone who looks on the Son and believes in him should have eternal life, and I will raise him up on the last day.' The 'I' is emphatic and is repeated several times. It is Christ personally who will raise up those for whom he died. Here is a glorious testimony to his love for his people.

The Bible shows us that there is the closest possible connection between Christ and his people, and so between their resurrections: 'the Lord Jesus Christ … will transform our lowly body to be like his glorious body, by the power that enables him even to subject all things to himself' (Phil. 3:21). We have a wonderful hope in union with Christ.

8

Raised in Glory

Our understanding of spiritual things is very limited. As the Holy Spirit illumines our minds in the study of God's word, we gain a knowledge of the truth, but our knowledge is so small compared to what there is to be known, and there is much that we will never be able to grasp. We are finite creatures, inevitably with limited capacity to understand the truth. Add to that the fact that our thinking is darkened by sin. Even when our minds are enlightened by grace, there is much that we do not understand, not least in relation to God's work of salvation.

Those limitations are very evident when we consider what the Bible says about the final resurrection that will take place at the return of Christ. In the previous chapter we considered the resurrection hope that Christians possess because of their union with Christ. It is crucial to understand that the Lord saves the body as well as the soul. Ultimately the bodies of believers will share in the resurrection glory of the Saviour. What those who have died in Christ now enjoy in heaven is not the full blessedness that the Lord has planned for his people. They will yet be raised with Christ.

God's revelation of that resurrection hope is wonderfully consoling for his people, particularly when they mourn the loss of loved ones, but it also raises many questions. Paul provides two examples in 1 Corinthians 15:35, 'How are the dead raised? With what kind of body do they come?' Those are questions that may well be in your mind as we continue our study of what the Bible says about the resurrection.

1. The necessity for our resurrection

We have already seen that the salvation provided in Christ includes the whole person. The body shares in his redemptive work and so must also share in its consummation. It will be raised from the dead. The Bible also sets out two other reasons why the resurrection of the body for the believer is a necessity, which we will now consider.

(i) *The resurrection completes our adoption.* A good case can be made for saying that adoption is the greatest blessing experienced by believers. Those who once were 'children of wrath' (Eph. 2:3), who deserved nothing but God's condemnation, are transformed into children of God. What blessing could be greater? As John puts it, 'See what kind of love the Father has given to us, that we should be called children of God; and so we are' (1 John 3:1). The same truth is set out in Galatians 4:7, 'So you are no longer a slave, but a son, and if a son, then an heir through God.' Adoption and the rights of sonship are a present possession.

There is, however, a future dimension to adoption. Believers do not yet enjoy all the blessings associated with adoption, but at the last day they will. This is evident in what the apostle Paul teaches us in Romans 8. Having described the effects of human sin on the material creation, leaving it in 'bondage to decay' (verse 21), Paul then speaks of the creation obtaining 'the freedom of the glory of the children of God.' There is a clear link between the renewal of creation at the end of time and the future glory of God's children. That this is bound up with adoption is made explicit in verse 23: 'not only the creation, but we ourselves, who have the firstfruits of the Spirit, groan inwardly as we wait eagerly for adoption as sons, the redemption of our bodies.'

The completion of the adoption of believers as children of God is bound up with their bodily resurrection at the return of Christ, which will also usher in the renewal of the entire creation. Here again we see the truth that our salvation in all its dimensions is always inclusive of our bodies. It is not some purely 'spiritual' experience.

This linking of adoption and resurrection is a further illustration of the 'already/not yet' pattern that we have noted in relation to the coming of the kingdom of God. We already enjoy the status and privileges of being God's adopted children, but not yet in their fulness. The resurrection will bring a new dimension to that relationship. In a richer sense believers will relate to God and serve him as beloved children body and soul, without the hindrances caused by sin. We may relate this to John's statement that 'when he appears we shall be like him, because we shall see him as he is' (1 John 3:6). It may be difficult to envisage how precisely our experience of adoption will be different, and it is probably far beyond our present ability to comprehend, but with all trace of our sin removed, the resurrection will complete our adoption and open for us the deepest possible relationship with God.

(ii) *The resurrection equips us for glory.* In 1 Corinthians 15:50 Paul states that 'flesh and blood cannot inherit the kingdom of God, nor does the perishable inherit the imperishable.' The present bodies we inhabit are not suitable for life in the new creation which will follow Christ's return. A new kind of life will evidently require a new kind of body. And that is what we shall receive, as Paul says: 'the trumpet will sound, and the dead will be raised imperishable, *and we shall be changed*' (verse 52).

The necessity for this transformation would appear to lie in the damage that sin has done to our present bodies. They bear the scars of sinful activity; they are returning to the dust from which they were taken and are subject to dissolution under the curse of God (as stated in Gen. 3:19). In bodily terms we are not equipped for the glorious life God has planned for us in his new creation. We will require new bodies, which will be graciously provided in the resurrection for all those who have died in Christ; and for believers still alive when the Lord returns there will be a comparable transformation (see 1 Thess. 4:16, 17).

Thus the resurrection of believers is necessary so that we will be able to experience and enjoy life in the glory of the consummated kingdom with the Lord himself. Body and soul, we will 'be with the Lord for ever' (1 Thess. 4:17).

2. *The nature of our resurrection bodies*

How does Paul answer the question which many Christians have asked with regard to the nature of the resurrection body? 'With what kind of body do they come?' (1 Cor. 15:35). He answers it by giving an illustration and then four contrasts.

(i) *An illustration.* To help us grasp something of the nature of the resurrection body, Paul uses the analogy of a seed and the plant that grows from it (1 Cor. 15:35-41). At heart this illustration teaches that the resurrection body will be both the same as and also different from our present bodies. Paul highlights two particular issues, one regarding the origin of the resurrection body and the other regarding how different it will be from our present bodies.

First, in verse 36, Paul writes, 'What you sow does not come to life unless it dies.' Regarding a seed, whilst it does not literally die, it can be said to die as a seed: it loses its initial identity in order to become something that appears to be quite different, yet in its new form there remains a strong continuity with its original form as a seed. That provides the point of comparison with the resurrection body. The present body must die (in its case, literally die and return to the dust). It loses its initial identity, but by the mighty working of God it becomes a glorious body which will appear to be quite different from the present body, yet there remains a profound continuity with its original physical form. Thus the body must die before the final resurrection is experienced. We might note that for those alive at Christ's return their bodies will not literally die, but will nevertheless be gloriously transformed (see 1 Cor. 15:51).

Paul continues in verse 37, 'And what you sow is not the body that is to be, but a bare seed, perhaps of wheat or of some other grain,' and concludes, 'But God gives it a body as he has chosen' (verse 38). The plant that grows is very different from the seed sown, yet there is a continuity between them. So it will be with the resurrection body. We cannot tell from an examination of the present body what the resurrection body will be like. It does seem clear from Scripture that there will be a continuity in appearance and recognition will be possible, as in the case of the risen Christ whose resurrected body bore the scars of his crucifixion in its hands and side (see John 20:25-27), but much is unknowable. Paul alludes to the variety of 'bodies' in God's creation—men, animals, plants, stars (verses 39-41)—and teaches that the resurrection body will have a unique glory all of its own.

(ii) *Four Contrasts*. These expand on aspects of the illustration.

(a) 'What is sown is *perishable*; what is raised is *imperishable*' (verse 42). Since the Fall the human body has been subject to disease and death. Inevitably our bodies return to the dust (Gen. 3:19). The resurrection body, however, will be free from disease and pain, no longer liable to death.

(b) 'It is sown in *dishonour*; it is raised in *glory*' (verse 43). The process of aging, with the decline of faculties and health, culminating in death by one means or another, is without any outward glory, even in believers. Even the fittest examples of humanity are decaying. The resurrection body, in contrast, will share in Christ's glory, being 'like his glorious body' (Phil. 3:21).

(c) 'It is sown in *weakness*; it is raised in *power*' (verse 43). The present body is weak in many respects and its capacities are severely limited. The resurrection body will be powerful—perhaps in regard to its health and its physical capacities, no doubt in ways we cannot now imagine.

(d) 'It is sown a *natural* body; it is raised a *spiritual* body' (verse 44). Paul is not suggesting that the resurrection body will not be material and physical. The word translated 'natural' (Greek, *psychikos*) refers not to the materiality of our bodies, but rather to their link with our fallen nature, our being 'in Adam' (called 'a man of dust' in verse 47). Our new bodies will still be material, as was that of the risen Christ, with 'flesh and bones' (Luke 24:39). Our new bodies will be 'spiritual,' empowered by the Holy Spirit and suited for our life in the new creation. Were the Lord to tell us more, we would probably not be able to understand him.

3. The nurture of our discipleship

There is a danger that these glorious truths could become matters purely for debate and speculation, a danger that Christians have sometimes failed to avoid. That, however, is not why they have been revealed to us.

The hope of resurrection should encourage *thanksgiving*: 'thanks be to God, who gives us the victory through our Lord Jesus Christ' (1 Cor. 15:57).

It should also be a stimulus to *holiness*: 'everyone who thus hopes in him [Christ] purifies himself as he is pure' (1 John 3:3).

It should result in *practical discipleship*: 'be steadfast, immovable, always abounding in the work of the Lord' (1 Cor. 15:58). The more we meditate and think about our hope of resurrection, the more zealous will our service be. The more truly 'heavenly minded' we are, the more 'earthly use' we will be.

9

Making Sense of 'the Rapture'

In times when the gospel faces concerted opposition and the church appears to be in decline—the circumstances in which the church in the West finds itself—it may be tempting to think how attractive it would be for Christians to be removed before worse days come. What if God were to spare his people from such terrible times as we find predicted in the New Testament?

When we read, for example, in Matthew 24:21 that 'then there will be great tribulation, such as has not been from the beginning of the world until now, no and never will be,' we may wonder if God would allow his church to pass through such terrible suffering before the return of Christ.

Some Christians would respond with confidence, 'He would not.' They believe that the Lord will remove the church before the final great tribulation, taking his people to heaven and to safety. They appeal to a verse such as 1 Thessalonians 4:17 ('we who are alive, who are left, will be caught up together with them in the clouds to meet the Lord in the air') as warrant for their belief in 'the rapture' of the church to meet the Saviour and go with him to heaven some years before his second coming. This event looms large in the eschatology of some Christians and so we must examine 'the rapture' in the full light of the whole Bible.

1. *What it is not*

Belief in an 'any moment rapture,' when all believers will be taken to heaven before the return of Christ, is characteristic of the system of theology known as Dispensationalism. This system was originated by John Nelson Darby (1800–82), a Dubliner who in 1827 left the Anglican priesthood and became associated with a group later known as the Plymouth Brethren. Darby's views of prophecy, particularly in relation to Israel's place in the purposes of God, were developed in a systematic fashion by a number of American Fundamentalists, of whom the most significant was the Congregationalist Cyrus I. Scofield. What may be termed 'Classical Dispensationalism' was given its definitive form in the Scofield Reference Bible, an edition of the Authorised Version with study notes, published in 1909, and in a revised version in 1917. The influence of Dispensationalism, in its original form and in later amended forms, has been very influential among Evangelicals in the United States and around the world.

According to Dispensational teaching there are two stages in the second coming of Christ: a coming *with* his saints at the end of history and a coming *for* his saints which takes place at an earlier point. It is the coming for his saints that involves what is termed 'the rapture.'

The main text cited in support of this belief is 1 Thessalonians 4:17. Having assured the Thessalonian believers that neither living nor dead Christians will be at a disadvantage when the Lord comes back for his people, Paul writes that 'the Lord himself will descend from heaven with a cry of command, with the voice of an archangel, and with the sound of the trumpet of God' (verse 16). Then 'the dead in Christ will rise first.' As far as living believers are concerned, 'then we who are alive, who are left, will be caught up together with them in the clouds to meet the Lord in the air' (verse 17). The entire church will be 'raptured' and will go to heaven.

So what will this rapture be like? Two characteristics stand out:

• It will be *sudden*: appeal is made to 1 Corinthians 15:51, 52, 'we shall be changed, in a moment, in the twinkling of an eye, at the last trumpet.' Both living and dead believers will be transformed instantaneously.

• It will be *secret*: the entire church will simply disappear, leaving, for example, cars without their Christian drivers. Believers will depart like Enoch—'he was not, for God took him' (Gen. 5:24)—here one moment, gone the next. Much is made of verses like 1 Thessalonians 5:2, 'For you yourselves are fully aware that the day of the Lord will come like a thief in the night.' It is claimed that the 'thief-in-the-night' language implies secrecy, and it has generated dramatic films and works of fiction from a Dispensationalist point of view.

This teaching about 'the rapture' is closely bound up with the view of Dispensationalists that God has separate purposes for Israel and the church. It is argued that when Israel rejected the Messiah, the clock of prophecy, as it is put, 'stopped ticking.' At present the church is being saved by God's grace in Christ, the Gentiles are being gathered in by the preaching of the gospel, but this work was not envisaged at all by the Old Testament prophets. The church, as far as Dispensationalists are concerned, does not figure in the Old Testament at all. At 'the rapture,' however, God will remove the church and again deal with Israel, probably before the tribulation and the rise of Antichrist. This will usher in the coming of Messiah's earthly Jewish kingdom and Old Testament prophecy will be fulfilled.

2. *What it is*

How should we respond to this view of 'the rapture,' which is often worked out in great detail? Close attention to the language used in the New Testament gives solid grounds for holding an alternative position.

Imagine a high dignitary, perhaps a royal official, is coming to visit a city in the ancient world. He would of course have to be afforded an appropriate welcome. Thus as he arrived, local officials would go out to meet the distinguished visitor and escort him back to their city. In the most public way possible the visitor would be welcomed and accorded appropriate honour.

That is the picture—indeed it is the language—of 1 Thessalonians 4:17, 'we who are alive, who are left, will be caught up together with them in the clouds to meet the Lord in the air.' The picture is of the Lord returning in glory.

The saints who are alive, and those who have already died (and whose souls have been with Christ in heaven), will all be part of these final events. The experiences of each will be different, with the dead receiving resurrection bodies and the bodies of the living being transformed to possess the same qualities, but none will miss out.

Note verse 16, 'the Lord himself will descend from heaven.' The greatest of dignitaries, the King of kings, is arriving to perform a work of judgment. He must be welcomed in the appropriate fashion. That welcome is what is being described in verse 17. The language used—'to meet the Lord'—is the language of such an official welcome. The resurrected saints and the transformed living saints will join in one vast company, the people of God in its entirety gathered for the first time, filled with joy and praise as they greet their Saviour-King. The whole church will form a kind of 'welcoming committee,' filling the role of local dignitaries in the welcome of a visiting official or ruler in ancient times. Every believer will share in that privilege, and Paul is at pains to emphasise the equality of the saints, living and dead, in performing this task. None need be anxious about somehow missing out or being at any kind of disadvantage. The blessing will be for each one equally.

What next? What will follow this 'rapture'? Despite the argument of the Dispensationalists that the church will return to heaven with Christ to celebrate the 'marriage supper of the Lamb' described in Revelation 19, all indications in the New Testament are that the next event in the Lord's eschatological programme will be the Final

Judgment. To continue the imagery of welcoming a dignitary, the returning Lord will continue to the earth. He will
not stop, turn around, and go back to heaven. The glorified
saints will accompany the Lord back to earth, where the
final eschatological events will unfold. This understanding
of 'the rapture' best explains Paul's words in the wider New
Testament context.

3. How does it fit?

It needs to be stressed that the return of Christ is always
portrayed in the New Testament as a single event, not one
that takes place in stages, separated by a period of years.
Thus his coming *with* the saints and his coming *for* the
saints are both parts of that single return.

• *Parousia* ('presence, arrival'): this is the word used of
Christ's return in 1 Thessalonians 4:15, 'the coming of the
Lord,' the event held by Dispensationalists to bring about
'the rapture.' Note, however, that the same word is used
in 1 Thessalonians 3:13 of 'the coming of our Lord Jesus
with all his saints' (not just those who have already died),
the supposed 'second stage' of the Lord's return in Dispensational thinking. In 2 Thessalonians 2:8 it is also the
designation of the Lord's coming at which he will destroy
the Antichrist—'whom the Lord Jesus will kill with the
breath of his mouth and bring to nothing by the appearance
of his coming.' The *parousia* is a single event.

• *Apokalypsis* ('revealing'): this is used in 1 Corinthians
1:7, 'as you wait for the revealing of our Lord Jesus Christ,'
which appears to be 'the rapture' of the Dispensationalists;

yet in 2 Thessalonians 1:7, 8 Paul uses it of the time 'when the Lord Jesus is revealed from heaven with his mighty angels in flaming fire, inflicting vengeance on those who do not know God and on those who do not obey the gospel of our Lord Jesus.' These again constitute a single event, the *apokalypsis* of the Lord.

• *Epiphaneia* ('appearance, manifestation'): this shows the same pattern of usage. In 1 Timothy 6:14 Paul charges Timothy 'to keep the commandment unstained and free from reproach until the appearing of our Lord Jesus Christ,' *i.e.* 'the rapture' of Dispensational thinking. Nevertheless, it is used in 2 Thessalonians 2:8: 'the appearance of his coming' (along with *parousia*) of the time of Antichrist's destruction.

With regard to all three terms, it is not possible to distinguish discrete 'phases' in the Lord's return—it is a single event. The language also serves to reinforce the New Testament description of the Lord's return as public and visible. The promise of Acts 1:11 is that he will return 'in the same way you saw him go into heaven.' Note Revelation 1:7, 'he is coming with the clouds and every eye will see him,' and the 'trumpet of God' (1 Thessalonians 4:16) indicates it will be an audible return. The thief of 1 Thessalonians 5:2 comes unexpectedly, not invisibly and secretly.

10

The Final Judgment

The injustice that we see all around us in the world often grieves us. The young, the old, the vulnerable are abused, sometimes to a scarcely believable extent. As news bulletins constantly remind us, the innocent frequently suffer and the guilty go unpunished, or indeed even prosper. Such a situation stirs a heartfelt cry such as Psalm 73:3, 'I was envious of the arrogant when I saw the prosperity of the wicked.' Having surveyed the apparent ease of the life of the ungodly, the psalmist joins with those who ask, 'How can God know? Is there knowledge in the Most High?' (verse 11). Many would echo those concerns.

These questions can relate to very personal issues on those occasions when we have experienced unjust treatment ourselves. It is no longer a distant or an abstract concern. It is significant that even those who would profess to reject all moral judgments sooner or later come to a point where they want to cry, 'That's not fair!'

There is something in us that seeks justice and that cannot be content to witness injustice. This is not merely a bit of idealism, nor is it the product of cultural evolution. It is, rather, a sign that the image of God in man, although defaced, has not been entirely erased. We have been made in the image of God—a God of justice—and we hunger to see justice done. That longing is not doomed to disappointment. A vital part of Christian eschatology is the belief that God will judge the world. Preaching in Athens, Paul states that God 'has fixed a day on which he will judge the world in righteousness by a man whom he has appointed, and of this he has given assurance to all by raising him from the dead' (Acts 17:31). The Final Judgment is approaching.

1. The timing of the judgment

It is clear in the New Testament that the judgment is bound up with the visibly glorious return of Christ. 'When the Son of Man comes in his glory, and all the angels with him, then he will sit on his glorious throne. Before him will be gathered all the nations, and he will separate people one from another as a shepherd separates the sheep from the goats' (Matt. 25:31, 32).

Although Matthew 11:22 refers to 'the day of judgment,' we need not assume 24 hours will be required. It may be completed in an instant.

2. The purpose of the judgment

In Luke 16:22-24 the rich man in Jesus' parable suffers torment and Lazarus is carried 'to Abraham's side.' In Luke 23:43 Jesus says to the dying criminal, 'Today you will be with me in paradise.' If the destiny of both saved and lost is known immediately upon death, why is the Final Judgment necessary? Both are known to God and he needs no enquiry. According to Scripture there are several aspects to the purpose of the judgment:

(i) It displays the glory and sovereignty of God in the revelation of the final destiny of each person. During the present age torment is experienced by the fallen angels (Jude 6) and the unsaved dead (Luke 16:23) and blessedness by the saved dead (Phil. 1:21-23). Those final states, however, are to some extent hidden. At the Final Judgment they will be revealed to the entire universe, to men and angels, together with the reasons for them. In the salvation of his elect God's grace will be manifested, along with the justice which required Christ's redeeming work. In the condemnation of the lost God's justice will be manifested, along with the common grace by which he gave them so many opportunities to repent. Both outcomes will reveal in a wonderful way the sovereignty of God and all will show forth his glory. No one will be in any doubt as to who is saved, who is lost, and the reason for each verdict. Central to the Final Judgment will be the glory of God.

(ii) It reveals the degrees of reward and punishment that each one will receive. The Bible makes it clear that there will be significant variation in both the rewards and the punishments that result from the judgment. Thus in Luke 12:47, 48 we read, 'that servant who knew his master's will but did not get ready or act according to his will, will receive a severe beating. But the one who did not know, and did what deserved a beating, will receive a light beating.' In contrast, in Luke 19 faithful servants are granted rewards proportionate to their service, described in terms of authority over ten cities and over five cities (verses 17, 19). In the Final Judgment God's perfect justice will be vindicated.

(iii) It assigns the final place in which each one will spend eternity, the final place of punishment in hell or the final place of blessedness in the new creation. The appropriate place for each will be eternally fixed.

3. *The agent of the judgment*

Who will carry out the Final Judgment? In the most general sense it can be said that the Judge is God. Thus in Romans 14:10 Paul says that 'we will all stand before the judgment seat of God,' and in 2 Thessalonians 1:5 we read of 'the righteous judgment of God.'

We can be more precise, however, since in the New Testament 'God' without further qualification often refers to God the Father. We can add to the references already given 1 Peter 1:17, which states, 'you call on him as Father who judges impartially according to each one's deeds.'

The Father is Judge, but we are dealing with the work of the Triune God. We must therefore also take into account Jesus' statement in John 5:22, 'The Father judges no one, but has given all judgment to the Son.' The Father carries out the judgment through the Son, with the goal 'that all may honour the Son, just as they honour the Father' (verse 23). To this can be added Paul's statement in Acts 17:31 that God 'has fixed a day on which he will judge the world in righteousness by a man whom he has appointed: and of this he has given assurance to all by raising him from the dead.'

If our view of Christ is to be properly biblical it must include the fact that he will be the Judge of all: 'For we must all appear before the judgment seat of Christ' (2 Cor. 5:10). The loving Saviour will also be the righteous Judge. As this text shows, the saved will also appear before Christ the Judge.

This is also evident in the judgment scene described in Matthew 25:31ff. It is a powerful description of Christ in his full glory. We are told that 'he will sit on his glorious throne. Before him will be gathered all the nations, and he will separate people from one another as a shepherd separates the sheep from the goats' (verses 31, 32). It is very clearly a royal work: this is 'the King' (verse 34). What is being described is the final consummation of his redemptive work as he completes the salvation of his people and punishes his unrepentant enemies. It is fitting that he should be the Judge. Those who are saved have been saved on the basis of his substitutionary atoning sacrifice and his victorious resurrection. This is the final stage of their salvation. Those who are lost are guilty of rejecting all possibility of salvation through faith in him, and so it is fitting that he should pass sentence on them. This is his triumph.

It is apparent from the New Testament that the unfallen angels and the elect will play a part in these events. According to Matthew 13:41, 42, the angels, as 'reapers,' will gather the lost and 'throw them into the fiery furnace.' According to 1 Corinthians 6:2, 3, 'the saints will judge the world …

we are to judge angels.' Apart from agreeing with the Lord's verdict, much of the significance of Paul's words remains hidden for now.

4. *The basis of judgment*

The basis of the verdicts passed at the Final Judgment will be the same for all, namely the revealed will of God. We noted above Jesus' reference in Luke 12:47, 48 to servants who knew and did not know their master's will and who received different punishments.

A qualification to this statement is necessary: judgment will be according to the knowledge of God's revelation which each individual had available. Thus in Luke 12:48 Jesus goes on to say, 'Everyone to whom much was given, of him much will be required, and from him to whom they entrusted much, they will demand the more.' No one will be judged by a revelation he did not have. Every human being possesses God's revelation in nature. As Romans 1:20 states, 'his invisible attributes, namely, his eternal power and divine nature, have been clearly perceived, ever since the creation of the world, in the things that have been made.' As a result, 'they are without excuse.' All also have the light of conscience, as Romans 2:12-16 shows. There is no suggestion that any respond positively to 'natural revelation.' Those who have the Old Testament have a revelation sufficient to point them to Christ, but they reject it in unbelief: 'If they do not hear Moses and the Prophets, neither will they be convinced if someone should rise from the dead' (Luke 16:31). Those who possess the full New Testament revelation will be judged by it. All will be judged with perfect justice.

The vital question is, 'What did they do with their knowledge?' When we read, for example, that 'the Son of Man … will repay each person according to what he has done' (Matt. 16:27), there is no suggestion that works can save any sinner. Actions reveal the heart and saving faith is evidenced by good works, as Ephesians 2:10 tells us. Works show the presence or absence of faith. They are a spiritual barometer. Romans 2:6, '[God] will render to each one according to his works,' in no way undermines salvation by grace alone. 'Whoever believes in the Son has eternal life; whoever does not obey the Son shall not see life, but the wrath of God remains on him' (John 3:36). Christ is our only hope.

5. The outcome of the judgment

As we shall see, there are only two possibilities, described in Matthew 25:33ff.

(i) *Sheep*. They showed their faith by humble service (verses 35, 36), not seeking to earn salvation. To them the Lord will say, 'Come, you who are blessed by my Father, inherit the kingdom prepared for you from the foundation of the world' (verse 34). They will enjoy 'eternal life' (verse 46).

(ii) *Goats*. The absence of service shows the absence of faith (verse 42-45). The Lord will say, 'Depart from me, you cursed, into the eternal fire prepared for the devil and his angels' (verse 41): words of irrevocable condemnation.

11

The Solemn Truth about Hell

When Myra Hindley died in 2002 the public response was remarkable. As one of the 'Moors Murderers,' probably the two most notorious child-killers in English legal history, Hindley's name is inextricably linked to cruelty and perversion. On her death, headlines in national newspapers proclaimed that she should, or would, 'rot in hell.' How striking to read such sentiments from the pens of journalists, many of whom would usually laugh to scorn any reference to the existence of hell. Yet some crimes seem to demand a hell.

Of course, for many people today, 'hell' is no more than a swear word, and not a very bad one at that. Few believe hell is a real place and fewer still expect to go there. And yet, as in the case of Hindley, they may think that certain kinds of people ought to go there. Something tells them that hell is appropriate for some offences, such as child murder. Clearly the image of God has not been entirely erased from men and women.

There are some sermons that a preacher would prefer not to preach, perhaps because the subject is difficult or embarrassing, or possibly controversial. He may expect a strongly negative reaction if he has to say things that he knows people will not want to hear. Such a subject is the doctrine of hell. Preachers prefer to avoid it and many do avoid it. If the doctrine of hell is in the Bible, however, preachers must preach on it and authors of Christian books on eschatology must write about it. It is clearly important and must not be ignored. We now turn to consider hell.

Since its earliest days the Christian church has held that the final state of the unsaved is eternal punishment in hell. In the eighteenth century a growing number of theologians questioned or denied the existence of hell and such reservations have continued into our own day. Some have opted for universalism, the view that every person will be saved. More have held to some form of annihilationism, holding either that man is created immortal and that gift will be withdrawn by God from the finally unrepentant, or that man is created mortal and that only the saved will be granted immortality ('conditional immortality'). Either way, the unsaved will simply cease to exist. The Bible's teaching is profoundly opposed to both positions.

1. Hell is real

On the basis of the word of God we have to say that hell is real. It is not a primitive superstition that we ought to have outgrown, nor is it a cunningly devised fiction, a means of social control designed to scare people into behaving in acceptable ways.

Many people are surprised to learn that no one in the Bible speaks of hell more often than the Lord Jesus Christ. He is certainly the perfect revelation of the love and compassion of God, but at the same time he had much to say on the subject of hell. To remove his teaching about hell would leave great gaps in the Gospel records.

Note first the Sermon on the Mount. In Matthew 5:22 Jesus warns, 'whoever says "You fool!" will be liable to the hell of fire.' He then speaks in verses 29, 30 of the radical removal of causes of temptation and sin using this striking language: 'It is better that you lose one of your members than that you whole body be thrown into hell' (verse 29). The word used for 'hell' is *gehenna*, which recalls the Valley of Hinnom outside Jerusalem where Ahaz and Manasseh offered child sacrifices (2 Kings 16:3; 21:6) and where the city's rubbish was burned in never ending fires.

Also significant are Jesus' words in Matthew 10:28, 'And do not fear those who kill the body but cannot kill the soul. Rather fear him who can destroy both soul and body in hell.' We will have to consider the precise significance of 'destroy' in due course. Note also Matthew 13:42, where the angels gather the lost and 'throw them into the fiery furnace,' and Matthew 18, where Jesus speaks of 'the eternal fire' (verse 8) and 'the hell of fire' (verse 9). Jesus believed that hell is real; and, we might ask, if his teaching on hell is rejected, why should any part of his teaching be accepted?

The same testimony to the reality of hell is found throughout the rest of the New Testament. In Romans 2 Paul warns sinners that 'you are storing up wrath for yourself on the day of wrath when God's righteous judgment will be revealed' (verse 5) and he goes on to refer to 'wrath and fury' (verse 8) and 'tribulation and distress' (verse 9). His language is particularly vivid in 2 Thessalonians 1:7-9. '… when the Lord Jesus is revealed from heaven with his mighty angels in flaming fire, inflicting vengeance on those who do not know God and on those who do not obey the gospel of our Lord Jesus. They will suffer the punishment of eternal destruction, away from the presence of the Lord and from the glory of his might.' Similar ideas are found, for example in 2 Peter 2:17 and Jude 13, and Revelation supplies numerous examples, such as Revelation 14:10, 11.

Throughout the Bible we find unanimous testimony to the reality of hell. It is a real place, though no indication of a location is provided. The language of 'going down' to hell should not be taken literally.

2. *Hell is just*

In Genesis 18:25 Abraham asks (knowing the answer), 'Shall not the Judge of all the earth do what is just?' God's actions are always 'just' or 'righteous'—either word would be an accurate translation—and that includes his judgment and punishment of sin. God 'has fixed a day when he will judge the world in righteousness' (Acts 17:31). In Romans 2:5 Paul refers to 'the day of wrath when God's righteous judgment will be revealed.'

Christians sometimes struggle to accept the justice of eternal punishment in hell. How could any sin deserve such consequences? Such struggles are often due to having too low a view of God's holiness and of man's sin. God is perfectly holy and all sin against him deserves punishment. To live life disregarding the Creator is the fundamental sin and deserves the punishment of hell. Those in hell never repent of their sin and so continue to deserve their punishment.

In a profound sense unrepentant sinners will receive what they have chosen, even though they did not realise the consequences of their choices. A life lived without God will lead to eternity without God. The Lord's action judicially confirms for eternity the choice that the sinner made in following his fallen nature. No one will be able to claim that hell is unjust. In all its awfulness it is exactly what sin has earned. That should serve as a solemn reminder of how wicked sin is.

3. Hell is terrible

The biblical descriptions of hell are powerful and vivid. In Mark 9:48, for example, Jesus speaks of a place where 'their worm does not die and the fire is not quenched.' The language of *fire* is frequently used. In Revelation 14:10, 11, which describes anyone who worships the beast and his image, we are told, 'he will be tormented with fire and sulphur in the presence of the holy angels and of the Lamb. And the smoke of their torment goes up for ever and ever.' The fact that such language is probably to be understood as figurative does not in any way reduce its power. These descriptions are the best way in which the Holy Spirit can convey to us in human language the awful prospect awaiting the unsaved. The reality of what these words portray will surpass anything the human mind has imagined.

Two elements of what hell entails will above all else make it terrible:

(i) *Separation*. The worst aspect of hell will surely be exclusion from the presence of the Lord and separation from everything that is good. This is clear in the Lord's words to the unsaved in Matthew 25:41: 'Depart from me, you cursed, into the eternal fire prepared for the devil and his angels.' The same truth is found in 2 Thessalonians 1:9, which speaks of 'the punishment of eternal destruction, away from the presence of the Lord and from the glory of his might.' This may also be the significance of the 'outer darkness' of Matthew 25:30. Separation is from the God with whom we were designed to enjoy fellowship. Without him there is no true life.

(ii) *Realisation*. The unsaved in hell will know the opportunities for salvation and blessing that they have spurned. This would seem to be indicated by the Lord's words in Matthew 13:42 regarding the fiery furnace: 'In that place there will be weeping and gnashing of teeth.' Here is revealed the remorse of conscience on the part of those who know why they are in that place and have lost all hope of escape. They will know what they have forfeited by their sin and the self-recrimination will be bitter.

4. Hell is eternal

The Bible is clear that hell lasts for ever. It offers no support for ideas of annihilation or conditional immortality. The punishment of the lost will be without end, not least because they will never repent, despite what they endure. They will always be in rebellion against God.

In making the biblical case that hell is eternal, we need to look carefully at two New Testament words:

(i) *Apollumi*: often translated 'destroy' or 'ruin,' or in the passive voice 'be lost' or 'perish.' In Matthew 10:28, for example, God is able to 'destroy both soul and body in hell,' and according to John 3:16 those who belong to Christ 'should not perish.' This verb never means 'annihilate.' In the parables in Luke 15 it is used of the sheep, the coin, and the son who are 'lost.' In Matthew 9:17 it is used of the old wineskins which are 'burst.' Even when it means 'kill,' as in Matthew 2:13 and Mark 9:22, it does not mean 'annihilate.'

(ii) *Aiōnios*: this is the word for 'eternal,' used for example in Matthew 25:46 for 'eternal punishment' and 'eternal life.' Some defenders of annihilationism argue that it means 'pertaining to the age to come' and has no implications for duration: the word is purely qualitative, not at all quantitative. We need not deny that *aiōnios* has qualitative significance, but we note too that everything associated with the age to come is in fact everlasting. The word does imply 'that which is without end.' It is used of 'eternal glory' (2 Tim. 2:10), 'eternal inheritance' (Heb.

9:15), and 'eternal life' (Matt. 25:46) of as long duration as eternal punishment. Hell is everlasting. It is a solemn truth to be preached faithfully and with love and tears, but it is a necessary consequence of the holiness of God and his perfect justice.

12

Christians in the Final Judgment

Perhaps you have had the experience of taking a wrong turning. Maybe you misunderstood the directions you were given, or you misread the map, or your Satellite Navigation System provided some wildly inaccurate instructions. Whatever went wrong, you did not arrive where you expected but instead found yourself somewhere strange. Perhaps you wondered, 'What am I doing here? How did I get here?'

At first sight it might appear to be a similar situation when a Christian—a saved sinner—finds himself standing before Christ the Judge at his return. Why am I here? What am I doing standing in the Final Judgment? Surely Christians do not need to be there?

The apostle Paul, however, tells us in 2 Corinthians 5:10 that 'we must all appear before the judgment seat of Christ, so that each one may receive what is due for what he has done in the body, whether good or evil.' Paul is writing to the members of the church in Corinth and he tells them that they must all appear before Christ the Judge. He even includes himself. How are we to square such a statement with the Bible's teaching about salvation by grace alone? How are we to understand references, such as Matthew 5:11, to rewards that will be given to believers? Can we earn God's blessing? If Christians are indeed to appear in the Final Judgment, there are several issues we need to consider.

1. Natural lostness

We need to begin our consideration of Christians in the Final Judgment by recalling what we are by nature. It is all too easy to forget that those who are saved by Christ were by nature no different from others. The description of Christians before conversion provided in Ephesians 2:1-3 should destroy any illusions about our natural spiritual condition. Paul tells us, 'you were dead in the trespasses and sins in which you once walked, following the course of this world, following the prince of the power of the air, the spirit that is now at work in the sons of disobedience—among whom we all once lived in the passions of our flesh, carrying out the desires of the body and the mind, and were by nature children of wrath, like the rest of mankind.'

It is a sobering description and needs to be quoted in full. Often Christians, especially if they have been raised in Christian families, can slip into thinking that it took only a small step for them to enter the kingdom of God. They may think that, however great the sins of others, their sins were less serious and perhaps required less grace to forgive them. Ephesians 2:1-3 tells a very different story.

Before conversion a Christian was not less of a sinner than others. He was dead in sin. He was not more susceptible to spiritual truth or to the gospel than others. In fact he may have been more hardened against such things than others, and may indeed have been a greater sinner on account of his resisting many godly influences on his life.

There is no place for spiritual pride regarding salvation. The fact that God 'chose us in [Christ] before the foundation of the world' (Eph. 1:4) does not mean that prior to conversion we were anything other than sinners. It was 'while we were still sinners, Christ died for us' (Rom. 5:8). Indeed, we were 'children of wrath' (Eph. 2:3)—we stood under the righteous condemnation of a holy God and what we deserved was 'wrath.' Left to ourselves, we would receive wrath at the Final Judgment.

2. *Gracious salvation*

How should Christians view their sin in light of the accounting at the last day? The key truth is to be found in a text such as 2 Corinthians 5:21: 'For our sake he [God] made him [Jesus] to be sin who knew no sin, so that in him we might become the righteousness of God.' Here is a clear statement of the substitutionary atonement made by the Lord Jesus Christ on the cross. Here is the heart of the gospel of grace.

This text indicates that the only way by which sinners may become 'the righteousness of God' is by reliance on the work of the Lord at Calvary. God's just sentence on sinners must be served: either it will be served by the sinner himself eternally in hell or it is served by Christ in his place. As the gospel tells us, the sinless Lamb of God has taken the full punishment due to the sins of his people, the elect of God. The righteous wrath of God has fallen upon the Lord Jesus Christ instead of upon his people, and so we can understand the agony he endured in Gethsemane with the prospect of the cross before him. The principle of substitution is crucial to salvation, and only the sinless Christ could be the substitute for us. As Paul says in Galatians 3:13, 'Christ redeemed us from the curse of the law by becoming a curse for us.'

As a result of the work of the Lord Jesus Christ, repentant, believing sinners receive a full salvation. In him God provides 'all things that pertain to life and godliness' (1 Pet. 1:3). Salvation is rich, much richer than some Christians realise. We receive in particular two blessings:

(i) *A kingdom.* Jesus' words to his sheep at the last day will be, 'Come, you who are blessed by my Father, inherit the kingdom prepared for you from the foundation of the world' (Matt. 25:34). Having entered the kingdom by the new birth (John 3:3, 5), God's people now enjoy the fulness of the kingdom. They will joyfully live for ever under the righteous rule of King Jesus, loving and serving him.

Scripture also indicates that there is a sense in which Christians will share in Christ's reign: they will reign with him. In 2 Timothy 2:12 we read that 'if we endure, we will also reign with him.' We are told in Revelation 22:3 that in the New Jerusalem will be 'the throne of God and of the Lamb,' and it is said of God's people, 'they will reign for ever and ever' (verse 5). We will be restored to the exercise of godly dominion in the new creation which was lost by Adam in Eden. The implications of that we can only imagine.

(ii) *Eternal life.* In Matthew 25:46 we are told that the righteous will go away 'into eternal life,' the fulness of the life which they have already received upon believing in the Lord. The presence and the possibility of sin will be removed and we will experience the life of the age to come. Covenant life in fellowship with God will reach its consummation, and the supreme joy will be that 'we will always be with the Lord' (1 Thess. 4:17).

This salvation is all of grace, the fruit of God's eternal love, from start to finish. The truth of salvation by grace alone is stressed throughout the Bible, not least in the familiar words of Ephesians 2:8, 'by grace you have been saved through faith.' All we contribute is the sin that required salvation.

A consequence of this is that in the Final Judgment our sins will be seen only as *forgiven* sins, covered by the blood of Christ, testimonies to the grace of God. Christians are sometimes anxious that their sins will be exposed to public scrutiny on that day, to their great grief and sorrow. We are, however, not to be confused by popular ideas of the judgment. The Bible does not suggest there will be a procession of sinners whose sins will be recited for all to hear. Such a scene would certainly inspire fear in any believer. We should envisage, rather, that Christ will deal with all simultaneously and each instantaneously. All the sins of believers will be seen to be forgiven and all the glory will belong to the Lord. We must not lose sight of Romans 8:1, 'There is therefore now no condemnation for those who are in Christ Jesus.' This is a powerfully liberating truth which lifts our burden of guilt and fear.

3. *Undeserved rewards*

It is a glorious thing to receive salvation as a gift of God's free grace. We never put the Lord in our debt. This is made clear by Christ in Luke 17, where he speaks of how a servant waits on his master, not *vice versa*. He applies the illustration in this way: 'So you also, when you have done all that you were commanded, say, "We are unworthy servants; we have only done what was our duty"' (verse 10). A lifetime of service is no more than what we owe the Lord who saved us. And yet there is more to be said about how the Lord treats his people.

The amazing truth is that the Lord loves his people so much that he, in grace, freely rewards them for doing what was their duty. He delights to shower his children with rewards for service which, as Matthew 25:35, 36 shows, he knows about fully. It is significant that when the Lord mentions their acts of service, such as feeding the hungry and giving drink to the thirsty, his people are amazed at his words. When they ask, 'Lord, when did we see you hungry and feed you?' and similar questions, it is clear that they did not do these things with a view to earning a reward or accumulating merit. They simply lived a gospel lifestyle.

In the course of his ministry Christ mentions rewards several times. In the Sermon on the Mount he says, 'Blessed are you when others revile you and persecute you and utter all kinds of evil against you falsely on my account. Rejoice and be glad, for your reward is great in heaven' (Matt. 5:11, 12). In the Sermon on the Plain he says, 'But love your enemies, and do good, and lend, expecting nothing in return, and your reward will be great, and you will be sons of the Most High' (Luke 6:35).

In Matthew 25:14-30, the Parable of the Talents, three servants give account to their master of how they have used money he entrusted to them. Two were faithful and are rewarded, one was not. The steward's wicked slothfulness demonstrated that his heart had never truly belonged to the master. The rewards, we see, are proportionate to the service, and the master's commendation is significant: 'Well done, good and faithful servant' (verses 21, 23).

How are such rewards to be understood? There is no doubt much that will not be clear to us until the last day, but it seems best to think of them as increased capacities to enjoy the Lord and to serve him in the new creation. Whatever the rewards, there will be no envy or discontent among the saints, but only praise to the Lord.

4. Necessary humility

Our response to such things must surely be that of David regarding the blessings of God's covenant: 'Who am I, O Lord God?' (2 Sam. 7:18). In contemplating what God has so graciously promised to do, humility is essential. 'What

do you have that you did not receive?' Paul asks in 1 Corinthians 4:7, and the answer is 'Nothing.' Thus we can face
the Final Judgment and look forward to the glories of the
new creation.

13

The New Creation

Most people have heard of *Paradise Lost* and *Paradise Regained*, even if they have not read a word of either. In his two great epic poems John Milton, one of the giants of seventeenth-century English poetry, sums up in grand poetic style the 'big picture' of human history. Beginning with the creation of the universe, Milton then goes on to describe the creation and fall of man and the provision for salvation made by God in the redemptive work of Christ. Whilst questions can be asked about Milton's theology, he works from within a Christian worldview and describes powerfully the transformation wrought by Christ in individual sinners and in the whole creation. The people of God can look forward to perfection.

It is striking that such ideas, including the hope of a future paradise, are not unique to Christianity. Many cultures, and the religions which have shaped them, have stories of perfection lost and regained, with the longing for a new world. Why are such hopes and longings so

common? Some might put them down to wishful thinking, born out of the hardships and suffering that people
experience in the world. With disease, loss, failure, disappointment, pain, violence, and all the other problems of
life, we should not be surprised by stories of a better world,
wishing it might be so. Is that all it is?

The Bible makes it clear that hopes for a better world, a
new world, are much more than wishful thinking. There
are, of course, many things for which we wish, sometimes
with an almost painful longing, yet we never come to possess or experience them. A better world, however, is not one
of those doomed hopes. In fact, as the Bible shows us, this
longing for a better world is part of the way in which God
has made us. As we might say in our modern, technological
culture, this is something for which we are 'hard-wired.'

The statement of Ecclesiastes 3:11 is profoundly significant: 'he has put eternity into man's heart.' We rightly see in
this verse a testimony to the fact that God has created men
and women with a desire for eternal life and for fellowship
with God which the Fall has not extinguished. It is a desire
that can be satisfied in Christ only. May we not also see in
the text an indication of the longing that God stirs in us
for a renewed, a transformed, an eternal world cleansed
of all the ravages of sin that we presently see around us?
This too is a longing that will be satisfied only in Christ.

When Christians think of their ultimate future, it is often
in terms of their being away from the world, translated to a
purely spiritual realm. Thus the thoughts of Christians are
generally of leaving the world behind and going to be in

heaven. It is not that they have forgotten the resurrection of the body, but they are unsure how it fits into God's plan, or perhaps they have never really thought about it. If this really truly is the shape of the future, it would appear that the material creation serves only a temporary function in the plan of God, needed until the last child of God is saved and then of no further value.

The Bible, however, gives us a very different perspective. It is certainly true that between death and the resurrection the spirits of believers are in heaven: they are 'away from the body and at home with the Lord' (2 Cor. 5:8). They leave this world and go to be with the Lord in heaven. But as we have seen, during that interim period believers are looking forward to the resurrection of the body as described in passages such as 1 Corinthians 15:12ff. The Bible tells us that the Lord will provide a suitable home for the resurrected saints. Not only will God's people be transformed, in body as well as spirit, the entire material universe will also be transformed. God continues to have a purpose for the creation: 'according to his promise we are waiting for new heavens and a new earth in which righteousness dwells' (2 Pet. 3:13). Here is the fulness of our Christian hope.

1. The creation shares in man's fallenness

If we are to understand the future of the creation, we must begin in the past, in particular with the fall of man into sin in the Garden of Eden. Having been placed in a perfect world, in uninterrupted fellowship with God, Adam, the covenant head of the human race, disobeyed

God's single prohibition and plunged himself and all his descendants into sin, under the righteous wrath of a holy God. The effects of that act are shown in the Bible to reach to every corner of creation, damaging every aspect of God's handiwork.

In Genesis 3:14 ff. the Lord spells out the comprehensive consequences of man's sin as he pronounces a curse on the serpent (Satan), on Eve, and on Adam. Every relationship of man is affected—with God, with his wife, and also with the material creation. As far as the latter is concerned, we read in verse 17, 'cursed is the ground because of you.' Human sin has a profound impact on the material creation and his relationship to his environment has become twisted and destructive.

What does that curse mean in practice? Among other things it means that 'in pain you shall eat of it all the days of your life; thorns and thistles it shall bring forth for you' (verses 17, 18). Instead of cooperating with man's work, the creation will resist his efforts to cultivate it, and so, 'By the sweat of your face you shall eat bread' (verse 19). The created harmony between man and the material world has been broken and ultimately death will have its say: 'you are dust and to dust you shall return' (verse 19).

We must understand that these are not simply natural consequences of the Fall, a kind of reverse evolution. It is clear from the record of Genesis 3 that all this represents a divine sentence passed on the creation. As verse 17 states, the ground is 'cursed.' The same truth is stated by Paul in Romans 8:20, 'For the creation was subjected to futility, not willingly, but because of him who subjected it.' The one who subjected the creation to futility is, of course, God. This is not merely a tragic accident: it is the will of a sovereign God, just as the Genesis account has demonstrated. The creation is now under a curse because of human sin. It is not now in its original perfection. Along with 'thorns and thistles' we can surely include diseases, pests, natural disasters such as floods and earthquakes, indeed everything in the world as it now is that causes pain and suffering, fear and death. The original harmony between man and nature has been destroyed and the creation truly is 'subjected to futility.'

Nevertheless there is reassurance in this. The state of the world is not the result of blind forces, nor is it ultimately controlled by Satan. The world is as it is because of the sovereign will of God, who is working out his glorious purpose. As we rightly grieve over the ravages of sin upon the creation, it is not a grieving that is without hope.

2. *The creation will share in redemption*

The Lord has not finished with the creation. As Psalm 24:1 reminds us, 'The earth is the Lord's and the fulness thereof.' That is still the case, despite the entrance of sin. He remains in sovereign control and it is his will that governs all things. He still 'works all things according to the counsel of his will' (Eph. 1:11). He will not allow his handiwork finally to be spoiled by Satan, and so he does not abandon his creation. Thus the material creation will share appropriately in the redemption which God provides for his elect. God places great value on his creation and at no point will Satan have a victory.

Christians are sometimes confused about this issue by a misinterpretation of a text such as 1 John 5:19, which states, 'the whole world lies in the power of the evil one' (literally 'lies in the evil one'). They conclude that in some sense Satan exercises control of the material creation. In fact that is not the case. Often in John's writings 'the world' is used in what we might term an 'ethical' or 'spiritual' sense, denoting fallen men and women in rebellion against their rightful King. They can certainly be said to belong to the evil one, living under 'the dominion of darkness' (Col. 1:13). It is in this sense that Jesus refers to Satan as 'the ruler of this world,' who is defeated by Christ's atoning death, an 'historic' event which also marks 'the judgment of this world' (John 12:31). None of these texts contradicts the rule of God over the material creation so clearly taught us in Scripture.

Paul's words regarding the implications of our redemption for the creation are very striking. In Romans 8:20 we saw that the creation was 'subjected to futility,' and the reason was 'because of him who subjected it, in hope that the creation itself will be set free from its bondage to decay and obtain the freedom of the glory of the children of God' (verses 20, 21). Gospel hope embraces the world, indeed the entire universe. It has a cosmic dimension which underlies the greatness of the power and grace of God.

We find the same truth in different language in 2 Peter 3:13, where, after a vivid description of cosmic transformation (verses 8-12), we read, 'But according to his promise we are waiting for new heavens and a new earth in which righteousness dwells.' The word for 'new' used by Peter (*kainos*) suggests a renewed creation rather than a fresh creation (for which he might well have used *neos*). Here is the fulfilment of a prophetic passage such as Isaiah 65:17: 'For behold, I create new heavens and a new earth, and the former things shall not be remembered or come into mind.'

Returning to Romans 8, it is essential to see that the context of the transformation envisaged is the redemptive work of Christ. Cosmic renewal is one of the fruits of what Christ has done in his life, death, and resurrection. Paul here makes a connection particularly with our *adoption*, the highest privilege granted to God's people. In verse 21 Paul states that the creation 'will be set free from its bondage to decay and obtain the freedom of the glory of the children of God.' He goes on to describe how both the creation and God's children are at the present time 'groaning.' Regarding believers, he says, 'we ourselves, who have the firstfruits of the Spirit, groan inwardly as we wait eagerly for adoption as sons, the redemption of our bodies' (verse 23). Already believers are 'children of God' (1 John 3:1), but there is a sense in which our adoption will not be complete until our material bodies share in resurrection glory at the return of Christ. Just as our material bodies will share in the benefits of the redemption Christ has secured, so too the material creation will have a share.

At the return of Christ there will be a reversal of the consequences of man's sin for the material creation, and the

Bible shows that it is this creation that will be renewed. The new creation will not be a fresh 'creation out of nothing,' as if sin somehow had forced God to scrap his handiwork. There is here a close analogy with our salvation. When God grants a sinner the new birth (John 3:3) he changes and renews that person: a new person is not created out of nothing. Thus Paul can write in 2 Corinthians 5:17, 'Therefore, if anyone is in Christ, he is a new creation. The old has passed away; behold the new has come.' It is the same person, yet a 'new creation' (again using *kainos*). The same is true with respect to the entire material creation.

This understanding of the renewal of the present creation is supported by the language of liberation used by Paul in Romans 8:21, rather than the language of annihilation and re-creation. His reference to the whole creation 'groaning together in the pains of childbirth until now' (verse 22) is also significant. The birth pangs indicate the hope of better things to come for this present world.

In the renewal of creation we see God's method for finally fulfilling Old Testament hopes regarding the land. In Hebrews 4:1ff. the writer describes Canaan as a foreshadowing (a 'type') of the eternal state. As he puts it, 'So then, there remains a Sabbath rest for the people of God' (verse 9), and he goes on to exhort his readers, 'Let us therefore strive to enter that rest, so that no one may fall by the same sort of disobedience' (verse 11). It is also significant that the same writer in chapter 11 considers the hopes of Abraham and the other patriarchs and indicates that they were not fulfilled by an inheritance in the present world. Rather, he says, they 'acknowledged that they were strangers and exiles on the earth' (verse 13) and ultimately 'they desire a better country, that is, a heavenly one. Therefore God is not ashamed to be called their God, for he has prepared for them a city' (verse 16). It is in the new creation that prophetic visions such as Isaiah 11:1-9 and Isaiah 65:17-25, depicting a renewal of the earth, will find their perfect and ultimate fulfilment. The hopes of God's Old Testament people never terminated on a piece of territory in this present world, but on the new creation, however limited their understanding of it necessarily was.

3. The creation will be transformed

As we have seen in Romans 8, the bringing in of the new creation will involve a glorious transformation of the entire universe. As Paul tells us, 'the creation itself will be set free from its bondage to decay' (verse 21). All the harmful and destructive aspects of the curse set out in Genesis 3 will be reversed. There will be nothing to harm or hinder the blessedness of the redeemed. As we read in Revelation 21:4, 'He will wipe away every tear from their eyes, and death shall be no more, neither shall there be mourning nor crying nor pain any more, for the former things have passed away.'

Romans 8:21 also states that the creation will 'obtain the freedom of the glory of the children of God.' The glorious resurrected saints will have a suitable home to share with the Lord. The greatest blessing of the new creation must certainly be: 'we will always be with the Lord' (1 Thess. 4:17).

The nature of this transformation is beyond our very limited understanding. Peter uses dramatic and vivid language in his second letter: 'then the heavens will pass away with a roar and the heavenly bodies will be burned up and exposed' (3:10); and in verse 12 he writes, 'the heavens will be set on fire and dissolved, and the heavenly bodies will melt as they burn.' It will be renewal of some fundamental kind, although not annihilation, but its precise meaning we can happily leave in the Lord's hands.

The question may be asked, 'Will we not be in heaven eternally?' The answer is, 'Yes.' Heaven is where God dwells. Thus heaven will embrace the new creation, where God will dwell with his people. In the language of Revelation 21, when the new creation is ushered in, 'I saw the holy city, new Jerusalem, coming down out of heaven from God, prepared as a bride adorned for her husband' (verse 2), and God says, 'Behold, the dwelling place of God is with man. He will dwell with them, and they will be his people, and God himself will be with them as their God' (verse 3), the fulfilment of God's covenant promise. 'The heavens' as part of the creation will be renewed: 'heaven' as God's dwelling place will embrace the renewed creation as the eternal home of his people. For those who belong to Christ this glorious future is certain.

Much about the new creation must remain mysterious. Our minds are so stained by sin, and our understanding so limited, that even if God had told us more about these things we could not have understood them. Nevertheless, the Bible reveals certain characteristics of the new creation which are more than sufficient to stir our hopes and longings.

(i) *Righteousness.* For this characteristic of the new creation the key text is 2 Peter 3:13, 'but according to his promise we are waiting for new heavens and a new earth in which righteousness dwells.' The new creation will be a place of perfect righteousness because this is the place where God dwells with his redeemed people. God is of course present everywhere in his creation. He is present in hell to punish the lost, but he is present in the new creation to richly and fully bless the saved. As Psalm 89:14 says, 'Righteousness and justice are the foundation of your throne.' Nowhere in the new creation will sin be found.

Everything in the new creation will be in perfect harmony with the righteous will of the Lord, everything in perfect conformity to his nature. All things will reflect his glory in every respect and there will be nothing to mar the holiness of this universe. That will include the redeemed, who will be conformed fully to Christ's likeness: 'we shall be like him, because we shall see him as he is' (1 John 3:2), a glorious prospect.

(ii) *Fulfilment.* In Romans 8:20 we are told that 'the creation was subjected to futility': other possible translations include 'emptiness,' 'purposelessness,' and 'frustration.' It is clear that the creation does not (yet) fulfil its potential as a result of man's sin. We too experience that sense of futility and frustration in many ways: in a fallen world relationships and work and all of life fall far short of what they could be. As the curse of Genesis 3 leads us to expect, much potential in the creation goes unrealised.

Last Things

In the new creation, however, we will experience comprehensive fulfilment. By God's grace his people will be all that he has designed them to be. In our activities there will be no sense of frustration or unrealised potential. All our faculties will be fully satisfied and our renewed bodies and minds will be able to enjoy God, our fellow believers, and the new universe to the full. There will no doubt be great scope for growth and development, but nothing will spoil what we do, and what we love—our love of beauty, of music, of many good things—will be fully satisfied. No one's life will lack fulfilment. That would seem to be the way to understand a prophetic passage such as Isaiah 65:20, which speaks of long life-spans before death in the new creation. It is a poetic way of indicating every life will be all it should be.

(iii) *Fellowship*. To be made in God's image is to be made for fellowship with God and with other people. It is profoundly significant that Revelation chapters 21 and 22 describe the new creation in the language of a city. It is also described as a cube (Rev. 21:16), like the most holy place in the temple. The city is a place flawlessly formed for holy fellowship.

The new creation will be a place of community, people dwelling together, a perfect community where the Lord's people enjoy fellowship with the Lord and with all his people. 'They will see his face,' we are told (Rev. 22:4). This fellowship is the fulfilment of God's gracious covenant: 'He will dwell with them, and they will be his people, and God himself will be with them as their God' (Rev. 21:3). It will

124

mark the culmination of God's eternal plan of salvation. Then we will experience in its fulness the delight of Psalm 133:1, 'How good and pleasant it is when brothers dwell in unity.' Nothing will spoil that unity.

(iv) *Beauty*. Sin has spoiled God's good creation, producing 'thorns and thistles' (Gen. 3:18), so that it is 'subject to futility' (Rom. 8:21). In ushering in the new creation God will reverse the effects of the Fall and will restore the beauty of creation. We may indeed expect that the beauty of the new creation will surpass anything seen in Eden. The language of Revelation 21 and 22 portrays vividly the glory and the beauty of the new creation using language that we can understand, such as the diverse precious stones of Revelation 21:18-20. The reality is beyond what human words can express.

The secret of the beauty of the new creation is that it reflects fully the glory of its Creator. He is a beautiful God, manifesting moral excellence and glory of every kind. Thus there will be no stain on the beauty of the new creation. Believers will share in that beauty. That will include their bodies, which will be like the glorious resurrection body of the Lord (Phil. 3:21). Everything will fulfil the Lord's plan for his universe. All will reflect his beauty: 'having the glory of God' (Rev. 21:11).

(v) *Security*. Life in this world is very insecure. Joys can pass suddenly, sorrows can unexpectedly beset us, life itself is liable to end without warning. In contrast the new creation will be a place of security. There the Lord will give abundant blessings that cannot be lost. The walls of the city described in Revelation 21 protect from all dangers, which are kept safely outside: 'nothing unclean will ever enter it, nor anyone who does what is detestable or false' (verse 27). Salvation could never be lost in the old creation, and in the new creation we will enjoy blessings that cannot be forfeited. We have the assurance that 'we will always be with the Lord' (1 Thess. 4:17) and we will enjoy 'an inheritance that is imperishable, undefiled, and unfading' (1 Pet. 1:4), the fruit of sovereign grace.

The prospects are glorious, but we must remember that they are only for the children of God. Those who are not saved by God's grace, who remain in their sins and are not 'in Christ,' will have no share in them. It cannot be stressed too much that it is absolutely vital to be saved and the only way to glory is through faith alone in Christ, as Paul said to the Philippian jailer in Acts 16:31, 'Believe in the Lord Jesus, and you will be saved.'

The future prospects of God's children should stir within them a profound longing and a sense of anticipation, which in turn should lead to 'lives of holiness and godliness' (2 Pet. 3:11). For all those trusting in Christ the best is yet to come!

'Amen: come, Lord Jesus' (Rev. 22:20).

Further Reading

Where to start

Edward Donnelly, *Biblical Teaching on the Doctrines of Heaven and Hell* (Edinburgh: Banner of Truth Trust, 2001)

W. J. Grier, *The Momentous Event: A Discussion of Scripture Teaching on the Second Advent* (London: Banner of Truth Trust, 1970)

William Hendriksen, *The Bible on the Life Hereafter* (Grand Rapids: Baker Book House, 1977)

David McKay, *A Christian's Pocket Guide to Humanity* (Fearn, Ross-shire: Christian Focus Publications, 2021), 4. 'Sharing Christ's Glory'

Derek W. H. Thomas, *Heaven on Earth: What the Bible Teaches about Life to Come* (Fearn, Ross-shire: Christian Focus, 2018)

In more detail

Jay Adams, *The Time is at Hand* (Nutley: Presbyterian and Reformed Publishing Co., 1966)

Oswald T. Allis, *Prophecy and the Church* (Nutley: Presbyterian and Reformed Publishing Co., 1977)

Graham Beynon, *Last Things: Living in the Light of the Future* (Nottingham: Inter-Varsity Press, 2010)

John Blanchard, *Whatever Happened to Hell?* (Darlington: Evangelical Press, 1993)

A. A. Hoekema, *The Bible and the Future* (Exeter: Paternoster Press, 1978)

Robert A. Morey, *Death and the Afterlife* (Minneapolis: Bethany House Publishers, 1984)

Christopher W. Morgan and Robert A. Peterson (eds.), *Hell under Fire: Modern Scholarship Reinvents Eternal Punishment* (Grand Rapids: Zondervan, 2004)

Robert A. Peterson, *Hell on Trial: The Case for Eternal Punishment* (Phillipsburg: P&R Publishing, 1995)

Kim Riddlebarger, *A Case for Amillennialism: Understanding the End Times* (Michigan: Baker Books; Leicester: Inter-Varsity Press, 2003)

Cornelis P. Venema, *The Promise of the Future* (Edinburgh: Banner of Truth Trust, 2000)

The bigger picture

Thomas Boston, *Human Nature in its Fourfold State* (1720; 1850; repr. London: Banner of Truth Trust, 1964)

Michael S. Horton, *Covenant and Eschatology: The Divine Drama* (Louisville and London: Westminster John Knox Press, 2002)

Frederick S. Leahy, *The Victory of the Lamb: Christ's Triumph over Sin, Death and Satan* (Edinburgh: Banner of Truth Trust, 2001)

David McKay, *The Bond of Love: God's Covenantal Relationship with His Church* (Fearn, Ross-shire: Mentor, 2001)

Herman Ridderbos, *The Coming of the Kingdom* (Nutley: Presbyterian and Reformed Publishing Co., 1962)

Michael D. Williams, *Far as the Curse is Found: The Covenant Story of Redemption* (Phillipsburg: P&R Publishing, 2005)

The Banner of Truth Trust originated in 1957 in London. The founders believed that much of the best literature of historic Christianity had been allowed to fall into oblivion and that, under God, its recovery could well lead not only to a strengthening of the church, but to true revival.

Interdenominational in vision, this publishing work is now international, and our lists include a number of contemporary authors, together with classics from the past. The translation of these books into many languages is encouraged.

A monthly magazine, *The Banner of Truth*, is also published, and further information about this, and all our other publications, may be found on our website, banneroftruth.org, or by contacting the offices below:

Head Office:
3 Murrayfield Road
Edinburgh
EH12 6EL
United Kingdom
Email: info@banneroftruth.co.uk

North America Office:
610 Alexander Spring Road
Carlisle, PA 17015
United States of America
Email: info@banneroftruth.org